MARKET LIKE A
HUMAN

Contents

4

Forward

On January 30, 2014, I started Bee Social, a social media marketing agency for small businesses. As an early 20-something with no experience starting or owning a business, I set out on my marketing and entrepreneurial journey with $2,000 and a lot of optimism — bright eyes, bushy tail, and all.

My journey into marketing is a unique one. I stumbled into it, but I am so grateful that I did. I always knew I'd own and run a business someday. I just didn't expect it to be so early in my career, or even in the marketing space. I didn't set out to run an agency. I didn't dream of being an agency owner. I didn't even think that someday I'd write a book. I stumbled upon marketing through jobs in high school and college and fell in love with it. I found a space to use both sides of my brain — the analytical side and the creative side — in most of my daily tasks. I also found a career that would keep me on my toes — I get bored easily. I'm always looking for a challenge, to learn something new, or to try out an innovative way of doing things. Agency life has given me all of that and then some.

Over the course of my nine years as an agency owner and entrepreneur, a lot has changed. We became a HubSpot Solutions Partner Agency in 2015, thus allowing the business to offer significantly more service options, such as content creation, SEO, website development, inbound marketing, account-based marketing, and more.

As a result of the expanded service offerings, we also decided it was time to rebrand because, let's face it, no one wants to buy a full marketing strategy and campaign retainer from "the social media guy." The Bee Social branding was fun at first but kicking the "social media guy" branding I brought on myself was one hell of a task.

We rebranded to HIVE Digital Strategy and have since dropped the "digital" from our name and now operate as HIVE Strategy (www.hivestrategy.com). HIVE Strategy, or HIVE, is now a team of more than 20 people who are smarter and more capable in their respective positions than I could have ever been alone. We are a Diamond HubSpot Solutions Partner, which puts us in the top 4% of all HubSpot Agencies in the world, and as of the time of this writing, we are currently on track for 11 straight record-breaking quarters. We also just completed our third consecutive year of more than 40% growth year-over-year.

None of this is where I saw myself or my agency going.

***

During my college days, I was managing an entertainment center in Colorado and interested in the business management and operations side of things.

As a business student, I planned to complete my Bachelor's and potentially go on to get my MBA, with the ultimate goal of owning and operating my own business.

In school I took a couple marketing classes that really caught my attention. I loved the idea that through messaging, cleverness, personality, and building trust, you could help people solve their business problems. It also presented me with an opportunity to tap into my creativity, which I found lacking in a business administration role. All of this meant that through my college career I bounced back and forth between getting a business management degree and a marketing degree. Eventually, I just got both.

With both degrees in hand, I needed to test my skills on the marketing side in a larger capacity. I had already proven to myself that, from at least a basic level, I could run a business (or that was my assumption as a 22-year-old — you know, the time of life when you think you know EVERYTHING).

To try out my marketing skills and determine if I could make a career in that field, I took a position as a marketing manager for a nightclub. Now, as those who know me can confirm, I'm about as far from a "nightclub person" as there can be. I have no interest in going to a nightclub, let alone working at one, but my theory was if I could be successful in marketing that nightclub, then I could probably make a career as a marketer (remember, 22-year-old logic).

I gave myself one year to "prove it." At the end of that time, the nightclub had its best year ever. My marketing campaigns and ideas were successful, and we were utilizing new marketing mediums the nightclub had never leveraged: web, digital, and social media. The owners had previously focused on more traditional marketing tactics like radio (tens of thousands of dollars just dumped into radio ads every month), flyers, billboards, and similar approaches.

After that one-year timeframe, I moved on and soon found myself interviewing for a role at a social media marketing agency. The interview process was terrible, but I had a flash of inspiration along the way: I could run my own marketing business. Again, armed with an early twenty-something's ego, I told myself that if the owners of that agency could run a successful agency, so could I.

Yes, the interview was *that* terrible.

I had just leveraged social media to significantly grow a nightclub and back in 2014, social media was far less competitive and more impactful in being able to grow a business. So, I decided to start a social media marketing agency.

***

HIVE Strategy has grown very quickly over the last few years, but that wasn't the case in the beginning. The early years were a grind. They were stressful.

They were flat-out hard. I was a first-time entrepreneur with no mentor, no entrepreneurial network, and no one to get real advice from. I learned lessons the hard way and I navigated the path myself. Most importantly, I had to learn all the principles in this book before I truly became a great marketer for my clients. It was a tall order and took many years to master.

At the same time marketing was undergoing a seismic shift, one that made much of what had come before completely irrelevant. When I started my agency in 2014, social media marketing was just catching on, social networks like Facebook and Instagram weren't limiting organic reach, and advertising on those platforms was extremely inexpensive. Since then, everything has shifted. More than once.

Today, the power, and I mean every last bit of power, is in the hands of the consumer and no longer the businesses. Consumers don't need us to tell them what to buy, show them the features, or preach to them about the benefits of our products versus our competitors. They already know. They're already doing their own research. Honestly, they don't even want to talk to us (at least not in the early stages). We just get in the way.

Because of this shift, we as marketers had to make a decision — would we continue to function under the (outdated) assumption that consumers need to talk to our salespeople, or would we change our mindset and focus on being a trusted resource for every stage of the process?

This conundrum led us to a path of quantity over quality and automation over personalization.

Today, marketers send millions of automated emails to thousands of contacts, pushing their value propositions and features hoping that someone, anyone bites. They don't care about the person receiving those emails. They probably don't even realize who is in the database they're blasting. The only thing they care about is *more*. More contacts, more lists, more clicks, more, more, more.

As a result, we find ourselves in an industry that feels sleazy. Marketing is viewed as a profession of pushing sales above everything else, regardless of what the customer needs. It's become annoying, intrusive, untrustworthy, and downright awful. It's become faceless.

We have to take a step back. We have to shift back to a focus on quality over quantity, authenticity over hype, effort over automation, and building trust over everything else. We can do better.

I'm talking right now to every single marketing person reading this book.

We can do better.

We *have* to do better.

But how do we do it? Unfortunately, especially in our current world, the answer is not quick or easy. It is going to take effort. It is going to take buy-in. It is going to take a shift in the way we view our prospects, leads, customers, and overall audience. It is going to require a reevaluation of everything we think we know about marketing.

But it can be done, and this book is going to show you how.

It all starts with being more human.

Thanks to my agency, I talk to hundreds of business executives every year. So many of them bring up the fact that they're a B2B (business to business), B2C (business to consumer), or a nonprofit organization as a distinction that is *the* vital characteristic of their marketing and sales plans. But what no one seems to inherently understand is regardless of whether you market B2B, B2C, or nonprofit — you're marketing to humans; real life people that are just trying to solve a problem. They aren't numbers. They aren't target accounts. They aren't faceless dollar signs. They're human beings.

We have to help them. We have to build trust. And if we do that, we will win. We will create brand promoters. We will grow our businesses because people will know us, like us, and trust us.

It's possible much of what I've explained so far feels slightly contradictory. I run a Diamond HubSpot Solutions Partner Agency. We, as I explain it to everyone I talk to, "Drink all of the orange Kool-Aid." HubSpot transformed the way my business operates and enabled us to be one of the best marketing agencies in the world. I owe a lot to HubSpot and we'll never move off the platform.

You may be thinking, however, "HubSpot is known for their automation tools, but you're saying automation isn't the answer." And you'd be right, to an extent. To be clear, I am not denouncing automation or marketing tools, nor am I opposed to creating scalable processes. I'm not saying you must sit down at your computer and personally craft every single email you send to a prospect or customer, or that you must do everything manually.

What I am saying is there must be balance.

Right now, the scale is completely tipped in the direction of automation. In the direction of simply pouring as many contacts as possible into the top of the funnel and hoping that something comes out at the end.

We need to even out the scale.

We need to regain some of the process and focus on being more human in our messaging, content, and overall marketing campaigns.

You can do both. You can have both.

But that means buying into the fact that humans respond best when they are treated like humans. They respond best when they trust you. They want transparency. They engage with personality. They demand authenticity. They understand consistency. They want to be helped, not sold. And they want to be part of a larger community. And those are the pillars of marketing like a human.

Are you ready to become a more human marketer? Over the ensuing pages, I'll share with you how to do just that. The exploration of each pillar ends with activities you can take back to your organization to instill a more human approach as soon as possible.

Let's take back marketing. Let's fix the industry. Let's be better. Because, let's face it, the world needs us to be. Our purpose is good — we, in some form or another, are helping people find solutions to their problems. But first, we must establish trust and build human relationships.

Let's go!

CHAPTER ONE

The Problem

The Sleazy Truth

Marketing has changed immensely over the last century and particularly the last decade. What worked 50 years ago, 10 years ago, even three years ago doesn't work today.

The root problem with marketing really began many, many years ago.

As we investigate what is wrong with the modern marketing industry, we first must take a trip back to the

"Mad Men" era. Back to using advertising to impact decisions, not based on the needs of the customer, but based on spamming, tricking, manipulating, and convincing mass audiences to purchase something they likely didn't need, based on a one-size-fits-all approach.

It was a world run by television commercials, radio ads, billboards, catchy headlines, sexy advertisements, and empty promises (both explicit and implicit).

Credit: Business Insider

The advertising industry was centered around its ability to manipulate large numbers of people to make a purchase. There was no effort to educate. No effort to build trust or a relationship. And definitely no effort to help a consumer make any decision that wasn't simply to purchase their product, and their product alone.

As outlined in *Manipulative Marketing*: *Persuasion and Manipulation of the Consumer Through Advertising*[1] by Victor Danciu, there are several levels of manipulation. In the early days, advertisers focused on the second stage of the spectrum of persuasion in advertising — manipulation — using deceitful tactics, fallacious arguments, and emotions to force decisions.

Table 1. *The spectrum of persuasion in advertising*

Coercition/Force	Manipulation	Rational persuasion	Factual information
Threat	Deceitful advertising	Logical arguments	Qualities
Physical violence	Fallacious arguments		Price
	Emotive persuasion		Display

Credit: Victor Danciu, Theoretical and Applied Economics 21.2 (2014): 591

Consumers purchased products because of effective messaging, promises, celebrity appearances, inaccurate or deceitful claims, emotional reactions, and great visuals. It's what they were supposed to do, right?

But the fact is the world in which these kinds of tactics worked is long gone. Today, thanks to the internet and the vast amounts of resources at the hands of the consumer, going down this road often ends poorly. There have been dozens, if not hundreds, of studies and surveys done that point to one truth: the power is now in the hands of the consumer.

They don't need our sales pitch, or even our sales team, like they once did. Not even close. They do their own research. They identify their own problems. They find solutions to those problems. They compare your solutions to your competitor's solutions. And once they're ready to decide between companies or services, they *might* reach out to your company for a sales conversation.

It used to be that a consumer had to talk to sales. They had to pick up the phone or drive to your business and have a high-pressure sales conversation about your products and services. Thanks to all the content, answers, and reviews currently available online, they don't need to do that. And, let's be honest, most of them (and us) refuse to do that.

We're not even buying cars in person anymore. We can find the car we want, fill out the paperwork, get approved for a loan, sign everything, and then schedule the vehicle to be dropped off right at our door — all online. Without talking to a single person.

This applies to an astonishing number of industries. Consumers don't fall for the tricks and manipulation that worked once upon a time. They're more sophisticated and they're armed with a plethora of tools and information at their fingertips.

Let's be clear — this is a fantastic evolution for the consumer. They can find the right solutions for their problems, answers to their questions, and the company, products, and services that fit all their needs on their own, rather than rely on the catchiest or most memorable commercial.

For marketers, it's a mixed bag. It provides us with an opportunity to be better. Both for us and for our customers. To be the source of answers and education. To be the relationship builder. On the other hand, it also can create distrust with our profession. And that's because consumers don't understand an important distinction, so let's get this out of the way now…

Marketing and advertising are two very different things

Advertisers are those who are willing to take your money, create those sexy ads, and focus on one thing and one thing only — dollars. Advertisers, like the Don Drapers of the world, don't care in the slightest about building a relationship with customers or helping them find any answer that isn't, "Buy my product." Advertisers and the sleazy tactics they have used since the start of time have created a distrust of all things advertising — and therefore all things marketing.

Don't get me wrong, advertising can be impactful and, if done well and implemented correctly within your marketing plan, can help your audience to find the solutions they need. There are good advertisers out there. But far too often, advertising is more focused on manipulation and tricks than actually supporting the people receiving those ads.

While the evolution from advertising to marketing has taken place over the last few decades, the public perception of advertisers spilling over onto marketers happened much more quickly. They think we are the new advertisers. People trust us less than an ambulance-chasing attorney, a slimy used car salesman, or the mall kiosk employee trying to grab your hand to pull you to their booth.

To be fair, some "marketers" deserve their reputation.

Organizations that only put out sales-focused content, constantly hit their entire database with sales emails, and gate all their content (just to force users to fill out a form to get any kind of useful information) are the problem. These organizations feed into the negative perception of our profession. Don't be that marketer.

At a time where we're re-examining and re-evaluating

our older institutions and how we function as a society,

the sleazy marketer is next to get the axe.

We have to take back marketing to be better for our

audience. At its core, marketing can be a helpful and

positively impactful profession. Marketing, in contrast

to advertising, is meant to build relationships, answer

our audience's questions, support them, help them

find the solution that is right for them, and above all,

educate them.

The world needs us — the real, authentic marketers.

The world needs our knowledge, platform, and

support.

Throughout this book, I will discuss the concept of how to take back marketing. I believe that the industry is broken, but it's important to note that taking back marketing is not just about creating bigger numbers on our profit and loss statements, or about dumping more and more leads into the top of our sales funnel.

It's about being a resource for our consumers, as well as getting out the messaging that applies to them and the content that they need. Crazy, right?

So, I begin this book with one important request — take this journey with me with an open mind.

Focus on not just being a more effective marketer to hit your KPIs and goals, but to create relationships with the *right* customers.

This book is not about how you can generate a million new leads or how to make an extra million dollars. It's about how you can become a better marketer for your audience. How you can be more effective in all your marketing through a human-centric approach. It's about understanding that regardless of who your prospects, leads, and customers are, they're people and people respond to human interactions and helpful information.

More, Always More

Stop for a second and answer this question for yourself — what is your top goal as a marketer this year?

You said something along the lines of, "Creating more leads," didn't you?

It's ok. That's what 95% of people reading this book just said to themselves.

This is how marketers are measured today. It's a constant focus on "more," always more: more leads, more contacts, more emails, more impressions, more, more, more.

Marketing has turned into a focus on quantity. We're measured by the number of leads we create, the number of followers on our social media pages, the number of website visitors, and the number of dollars we're helping to generate. But how effective is this focus for our companies?

With this quantity-focused mentality, we don't care about who we're reaching, just that we're reaching them. We don't care who is following us on social media, just that they are following us. We don't care about who is on our email list, just that they open our email blasts.

See the problem?

The focus on quantity directly contrasts with what consumers want us to be. Instead of thinking about how you can send more emails, get more impressions, or clickbait more people into coming to your website, we must change the narrative to engage the right people, at the right time, through the right channels, with the right messaging.

Engage the right people, at the right time, through the right channels, with the right messaging

Making a shift from the quantity-focused mentality to a quality-centric approach allows us to be significantly more effective, helpful, and supportive for our audience. And while it is not focused on the same "more, more, more" goals, it will assist more of the *right* people and customers in finding and working with us.

As I'm writing this, we just went through the holiday season with all the Black Friday deals, holiday sales, and end-of-year discounts. It's always a crazy time of year for marketers, where we focus on pushing those end-of-year sales. It's also the most annoying time of the year for marketing.

I look at essentially everything that comes to me — whether it's through snail mail, email, television, in-app, whatever — from a marketing perspective. I think about what the intent was, why I personally received that message, and what the marketer's strategy may have been.

During the holiday season, it seems as though almost every marketer in the world simultaneously goes into a trance and reverts to the old advertising tactics. It's like they forget about the relationship building and educational side of their work and solely focus on persuading customers to buy their widgets. We're all bombarded with sales messaging — even if it has nothing to do with us or our interests.

I could probably pull up dozens of examples just from this last holiday season alone, but one stands out in my mind.

I have purchased a lot of items over the years from Best Buy (I can neither confirm nor deny that I have a bit of a technology obsession). Over the last year I have purchased a television, two monitors, a Mac Studio, Apple Airpods, a phone case, and screen protector for my iPhone from Best Buy. (Apple problem? I don't have an Apple problem. You have an Apple problem!) All of this was done using my Best Buy account and email address. You'd think that would give the company a solid grasp of who I am, what I'm interested in, and how to promote sales and new products to me.

That was decidedly *not* the case this holiday season. In November and December alone, I received a total of 59 emails (more than seven emails per week) from Best Buy.

First, that is wildly spammy. No one wants to receive more than one email every day from *any* business. It's overkill and completely obnoxious.

On top of that, Best Buy compounded the issue by not delivering any sort of segmented or customized experience using what they already knew about me. Based on my purchase history alone (not even going into the products that I have looked at online), they should be aware of what model of iPhone I have, my affinity (or addiction) for Apple products, and that I likely do a lot of work on my computer. Emails about Apple sales and new products, upgrading my iPhone, and accessories for my devices and workspace would be very relevant to who I am and what I'm interested in.

Those kinds of messages would speak to my interests, not the interests of what Best Buy wants to sell me.

Instead, I received an email every single day about sales on gaming equipment, appliances, projectors, fitness equipment, virtual reality headsets, air purifiers, cameras, and just about everything else that I have no interest in. There was absolutely no personalization to these emails. I was just another email in their database.

As I mentioned earlier, I read all these marketing emails and communications because they're interesting to me from a marketing perspective. For these messages, I tried to get into the mind of the marketers who decided this strategy was a good idea. I tried. I really did. I tried to understand what they were thinking. I tried to understand why they didn't use any sort of personalization token in a single email. I tried to understand why almost every one of the 59 emails looked nearly identical. I tried to understand why they thought, based on my purchase and website activity history, that I wanted ads for gaming systems, Samsung watches, and Windows laptops. I tried and tried, and at some point my brain simply clocked out and I came to in a dive bar in San Bernardino. No idea how I got there.

Ok, no I didn't, but I definitely could have used a drink after those two months.

Not only was this entire campaign lazy, with an almost identical design each time and no thought put into the actual content of the emails, but it made me feel like a number. It led me, as a consumer, to an obvious conclusion — Best Buy doesn't care about me as a human. They only care about me as far as my wallet will take me. They only care about getting me to purchase something, anything, from them this holiday season.

It was infuriating and annoying. But the most infuriating and annoying part of all was the insane level of spam. It has made me reconsider where I purchase my technology. Maybe Amazon is the way to go. Amazon does a great job of understanding what I'm interested in and showing me that content and those products. Best Buy apparently hasn't figured that out.

Best Buy clearly subscribes to the more, more, more mentality. They were focused on one thing and one thing only — new sales. Those emails weren't meant to do anything but throw as many ads in my face as possible.

This is not how organizations will win moving forward. We tune these things out. And even with as much money as I have spent at Best Buy over the years, I unsubscribed from their emails because they were so annoying.

Do better, Best Buy. And if you've recently subscribed to this kind of tactic during the holiday season or at any point during the year, it's time for you to reconsider your strategy and do better as well.

This isn't marketing. This is blind advertising at its worst.

How to Know If You Have a Marketing Problem

There are several ways to identify if you have a marketing problem, and honestly, most organizations have some kind of issue lingering in their plans. Sometimes it's a full-blown epidemic within their organization and in others it's a small issue that rears its ugly head every once in a while.

The most obvious red flags are a quantity-only focus on key performance indicators and goals, a lack of regular educational content (and I'm talking more than 50 new pieces of content per month between social media, blogging, website content, emails, landing pages, etc.), overly-gated content, and a sales team that says all the leads they're getting are "bad."

Let's dive a little deeper into each of these issues and why it signals a marketing problem.

Quantity-Only Focus

A quantity over quality focus is good for no one. I talk with organizations all the time that only want to buy a list of 50,000 contacts so they can send (spam) their messaging to them. You know what happens to those organizations? They get blacklisted, unsubscribed, marked as spam, and completely ignored by anyone who may have been a good prospect. They lose all trust with that list and immediately fall into that negative category, with the sleazy salesmen and advertisers of the past.

As a (good) marketer today, you can't solely be focused on quantity metrics. And, believe me, that isn't always easy. There's a lot of pressure from above and from the sales team to constantly produce more and more leads.

Consider this — what good is getting more leads if they're all terrible fits? Or producing more website visits if they all just bounce off the page and never come back?

As the marketing team, we must make the time to not only educate our prospects, leads, and customers, but also educate our internal teams and stakeholders on the importance of pivoting to quality-focused metrics, goals, and key performance indicators.

If you're currently in this boat, think about it — is your marketing strategy really producing what you want it to? What does your conversion rate look like? What does your close rate look like? Are you pushing more people to your website just to have them all bounce away?

Sharing website visits, social media followings, clicks, and other vanity metrics only really accomplishes one thing — it makes us feel good. They don't signal business growth or success.

Instead, we should focus on metrics like meetings booked, subscriptions, form fills, deals created, and impacted revenue to truly understand the impact of our marketing efforts and initiatives. These metrics testify to the quality of the leads we're generating and engaging with, rather than the quantity.

While a large number looks fantastic on a report, the actual quality is best demonstrated on a profit and loss statement and through repeat customers.

Lack of Regular Educational Content

Earlier when I touched on this point, I mentioned more than 50 new pieces of content per month. You might still be picking your jaw up off the floor. That's ok. Take your time.

I know 50 new pieces of content per month sounds like an insane amount. But that is truly what it takes to educate and build a relationship with your audience.

I am not saying you have to produce 50 new eBooks and white papers each month, but I am saying you should be delivering a variety of content in different formats to your targeted and segmented audiences each month to support their journey.

Content takes many forms. It could be social media posts across your different platforms, newsletters and emails segmented based on the interests of your audiences, or downloadable content like eBooks, white papers, infographics, or checklists. It could also be videos, new landing pages and website pages, or even blog posts and educational articles.

Your medium for delivering content should depend on what your audience likes and wants to engage with.

But whatever the selected mediums are, you should actively produce a regular stream of new, helpful content for that audience.

Once you really consider it, 50 new pieces of content really isn't *that* much. Examining the content we produce each month for HIVE Strategy, our breakdown looks something like this:

- 10-15 blog posts
- 15-20 business social media posts across LinkedIn, Twitter, Facebook, and Instagram
- 10-15 social media posts from my personal profiles on LinkedIn and Twitter
- 2-3 new pages (landing pages, website pages, updated pages)
- 5-7 emails

Add to the list the sporadic press release, podcast, video, guest post, and interview.

All this content is filed into a content calendar with the specific purposes of supporting, educating, and building relationships with the right prospects, leads, and customers for our business.

You may not have noticed it a couple pages ago, but I mentioned a critical word in relation to the content you should be producing — *helpful*.

This is not sales content.

I repeat — the content we are talking about (the more than 50 pieces of content) is **NOT** sales content.

They are pieces of content geared towards helping your audience in their research, education, and evaluation processes. They are focused on helping your audience:

- Identify their problems.
- Work out possible solutions to those problems.
- Get better at their jobs.
- Evaluate solutions to determine their best course of action.
- Determine which product, service, or provider fits their needs best.

They are not geared towards scheduling a sales call or buying a product — at least not immediately.

There is absolutely a place for sales content, but that should be in addition to these 50 pieces geared toward education. Sales content can take the same form as your educational content (social media posts, advertisements, blog posts and articles, videos, podcasts, etc.), but it should not be lumped into the same category. Sprinkle these pieces of content throughout the month, in between your helpful content, and you'll find your sales content becomes significantly more impactful. The reason? You're taking the time to build rapport and a relationship with your audience, and making that the priority.

Overly-Gated Content

This issue stems directly from the quantity-focused mentality behind most modern marketing campaigns.

We need to produce more leads for our sales team and therefore we must require more people to fill out forms. In fact, we *need* them to fill out those forms so we can reach our unrealistic lead goals and expectations.

You can see the solution many organizations employ coming a mile away — just gate *everything* behind a form. In order to get any valuable information from our organization, we tell our visitors that they need to give us something. They need to share their information so we can spam the absolute crap out of them, until they either get fed up and unsubscribe/block us, or finally make a purchase.

What a great plan.

And so, we gate our resources. We gate our case studies. We gate our articles. We gate our downloadable content. We gate our videos. We gate our bathrooms. We gate our oxygen. We gate anything that has any value at all.

I have had the gating conversation with clients about a million times by now. So many organizations think if they are going to take the time to produce good, quality content, the visitor should essentially have to pay for it with their information. We need visitors to give us something for the time we put into creating that content; for sharing our knowledge.

The problem is our audience doesn't care.

Who cares that it took you 20 hours to produce that eBook?

Only you.

Only your business.

Your audience doesn't care about your level of effort. They only care about how your content supports their needs and helps them solve their problems. You need to get past the amount of time and resources you have invested in your content and understand that the purpose of 90% of your content shouldn't be to simply get someone to fill out a form. It should be to help them — and help them without immediately expecting something in return.

Your audience doesn't care about your level of effort. They only care about how your content supports their needs and helps them solve their problems.

I work with a client who required a great deal of help to get their mind around this principle. When they came to HIVE, everything on their website was gated. And when I say everything, I mean EVERYTHING. Visitors couldn't access more than 150 words of any blog post without having to subscribe. Visitors couldn't watch any of their hundreds of videos without filling out a form. Visitors couldn't even see their case studies without giving up their email address.

This was my client and even I was annoyed going to their website. It focused solely on their business, with no regard for helping their audience and website visitors.

The worst part was their content was actually really good. They spent a lot of time producing great, helpful materials, but because they decided being helpful to their audience was less important than forcing them to convert, they lost a lot of trust with their prospects and even with their customers.

They took a lot (and I mean *a lot*) of convincing to scale back the gating. We finally persuaded them to open up their blog and provide an option for people to subscribe, but it wasn't a requirement to access any of their content. They ungated their case studies and promoted them to segmented audiences as social proof and trust-building content (which happens to be the entire purpose of a case study — who knew?). They began sharing their videos everywhere (social media, email, on their website, in their blog, and on their YouTube channel). They still kept some of their high value content gated (mostly eBooks and white papers), but the majority of their content was transformed from sales-focused, with the strict purpose of converting a lead, to helpful content — just by un-gating the material.

The results? They had the best year in the company's history. They were able to increase the number of quality sales conversations, meetings booked, and even regularly received feedback on their content from prospects during those sales conversations. All because the company was so helpful.

A shift in mentality lead to audience rewards. The company attracted, engaged, and converted the right people into leads at the right time. Finally, they understood that humans don't want to be forced into anything. They don't want to be hard sold. They want to learn. They want to be helped. And they want to be respected.

Somebody please cue Aretha Franklin.

"Bad" Leads

If I'm being completely honest, this one makes me crazy.

First, because I'm a marketer and the finger pointing from sales saying, "Marketing isn't delivering good leads," is one of the worst cop-outs.

Second, because, well, they're probably more right than wrong.

If we focus on creating as many leads as humanly possible, that generally results in poor overall leads. It means we're focused on fulfilling some unreasonable and unrealistic expectation of lead generation and the only way to do that is to get anyone that you possibly can to become a lead.

"Bad" leads mean we didn't take the time to truly understand our prospects, their needs, or the actual people behind them.

"Bad" leads mean we've forced a sales conversation before these people were ready for that conversation.

"Bad" leads mean we didn't do enough upfront in our marketing to educate our audience about what we do, how it helps them, and why we are (or aren't) a good fit for them.

One gigantic mistake I see many businesses make is they think every single conversion is a sales conversion. What I mean is that if someone simply downloads your eBook, they're probably not ready to be bombarded with sales messages. If someone only subscribes to your blog, they're probably not expecting a phone call from your sales team. If someone fills out the form on your website calculator just to see the final result, they're probably not standing by with their credit card waiting for you to ask them for those numbers.

Somewhere along the line, the definition of sales stages was completely blurred and turned into a free-for-all, where any time someone fills out any form or engages with us in any way, we think that signals that they're ready to buy from us. Again, this returns to our constant need for more.

Instead of turning your potential leads off and running them away using overly aggressive and unexpected sales barrages, take the time to understand what that person expects out of the engagement with your organization.

If they fill out your blog subscription form, they're likely just looking for more educational and helpful content to support their job, their research, or their overall education around your industry and organization.

If they fill out a form for an awareness stage (when someone is just starting to identify that they have a problem and what it is) eBook download, they're probably just trying to better understand their problem. Again, they're looking to be educated.

Neither of these situations should scream "sales" to you or your organization. In fact, neither of these leads should get anywhere near a salesperson at this stage. These leads are meant to be nurtured. These leads are in an educational mindset, not a purchasing mindset. Respecting and understanding the difference between these mindsets will mean the difference between an eventual sale and a blocked salesperson.

So, my question here is this: is marketing *really* delivering "bad" leads? Or are those leads just not ready to be sold? There is a big difference between a truly "bad" sales lead and one that shouldn't have been a sales lead in the first place.

What is Marketing? What is it Becoming?

Now we come to the big question. But first, I want to talk about what marketing is *not*.

Marketing is *not* purchasing lists of contacts that have no idea who you are.

Marketing is *not* blasting your entire database with a generic sales message.

Marketing is *not* purchasing Instagram followers.

Marketing is *not* creating clickbait content with the sole purpose of getting clicks to your website or blog.

Marketing is *not* creating content that only talks about your business.

Marketing is *not* sharing only sales-focused content.

Marketing is none of these things, because, if there's one thing marketing should be, it's helpful.

If there's one thing marketing should be, it's helpful.

It's about helping people find the solutions to their problems. It's about engaging with the right people, at the right time, through the right medium, when they need you most. It's about being seen, recognized, and understood by your audience, not because you interrupt or bombard them with spam, but because you have created the content they need. You have the content that answers the questions they're asking (even if those questions are difficult or taboo in your industry).

Marketing is meant to be fun, engaging, educational, and memorable. The most effective marketers understand who their audience is, where they spend their time, who they're marketing to, and how they want to consume their content.

Marketing isn't meant to be intrusive or spammy. It isn't advertising. It shouldn't show up when it's not expected. And it shouldn't focus on sales (that's the sales team's job).

We must return to what marketing was always meant to be. We must understand that marketing creates a relationship with our audience, which then creates an affinity with our brand which, through nurturing and consistently helpful content, creates sales-qualified leads that are then ready for a sales conversation.

Throughout this chapter I have written about creating leads and the mistreatment of those leads. To be clear, I am absolutely not against using forms or any lead-generating activity. I am, however, against the abuse of forms and the abuse of people that made the mistake of converting on those forms.

If you're only focused on getting someone to fill out a form in order to immediately push that person to sales — you're not marketing. You're embodying the old school advertising mentality. You're closer to the Don Drapers of the world than to the Neil Patels (of NP Digital), Rand Fishkins (of SparkToro, formerly of Moz), or Ann Handleys (of MarketingProfs).

Take a second to think about your process and if it aligns with the goals and expectations of your leads. What are those people expecting to happen next? How can you fulfill that expectation?

Activity

Now that we've gone through the problem with marketing today, it's time to think about where you and your organization stand:

1. Pull together a list of your goals for this month, quarter, and/or year and think about how you can improve them so they're more heavily focused on quality over quantity.

    a. If you're part of a larger team, discuss with the entire group what a transition to a quality-focus looks like and how you can incorporate that into your marketing and sales expectations moving forward.

2. Run a content audit to determine how much of your content is sales-focused versus helpful.

    a. Additionally, ascertain how much of your content is gated and how much you're asking for from your users. Think about what could be ungated, what could be repurposed, and which forms you may be able to reduce to lower the barrier to entry.

3. Review your form process to determine how and when a lead is being sent to a salesperson and determine whether that lead would be expecting, or even ready for, a sales conversation, or if they were just looking for helpful resources.

4. Talk with your sales team to determine why the leads they're being delivered are "bad" and how you can improve their quality.

5. Review some impactful marketing campaigns you've seen recently, whether in your industry or that you've seen as a consumer, and determine what you liked and didn't like about the campaigns and content.

    a. Once you've reviewed these campaigns as a team, brainstorm how you could implement something similar for your organization's work and how it can impact and resonate with the humans who receive your messaging.

[1] Victor Danciu, Theoretical and Applied Economics 21.2 (2014): 591

CHAPTER TWO

Transparency

As business owners, marketers, and sales reps, we naturally want to talk about the good things: the things that make us stand out and paint our organization in a positive light. But rarely (if ever) do we talk about anything that does the opposite. It's human nature to only focus on the good and ignore the bad, but let's be honest — our consumers want the dirt, or as the kids say, the tea.

They want to know *all* the good as well as *all* the bad before they make a purchasing decision.

The problem, for the consumer, is finding the bad is often difficult or inaccurate. It usually comes from reviews and competitors, not from the company with which they're considering working.

Now, I say "bad," but it's not really bad.

I am not suggesting you pull every skeleton out of your closet and put it on display for the whole world to see. What I am suggesting is providing more transparency into your business, your operations, pricing, and who you do and do not work with. This can be immensely helpful for your prospects. And if you are the one giving that information, you're able to control the narrative and *you* become a trusted resource and authority in the eyes of your consumers.

Let's explore a few ways you can start being more transparent with your audience and take a giant leap ahead of your competitors when it comes to marketing like a human.

Pricing

One of the top questions I get from new clients and prospects is, "Do I *need* to share pricing on my website?" My response is always, "When you are researching something to buy, how does it make you feel when you go to a company's website and search for pricing, but can't find it?"

We can all answer together: **it sucks**, right?

So, why would you create that kind of feeling for your consumers? It doesn't make any sense.

We are part of a society that loves to do our own research. According to recent studies, up to 90% of the sales cycle is complete before a prospect ever reaches out to your company or salespeople[1]. What this tells us is that in order to win, we must provide the information consumers are looking for, when they're looking for it. And at the very top of most customers' lists is pricing.

Consumers need to not only know how your company, products, or services solve their problems, but also whether your solutions fit within their budget. If they have a Toyota Camry budget, they're not going to be interested in your Lamborghini Aventador solution (no matter how pretty, shiny, and fast it is).

Let's stick with that car metaphor for a second. You'd never go looking for a car and not filter by price, right? Think about how that would look — you visit Cars.com or Auto Trader and search for any kind of car within 500 miles of you. What would you get? You would see 20-year-old cars for $5,000 with 200,000 miles and you would also see $250,000 super-cars, and everything in between. The people looking for these two disparate types of cars are very different people and are interested in very different things.

Why aren't we embracing this truth? Why are we making people guess whether our products and services are actually within their budget?

The same holds true for people researching marketing agencies to work with. The person who has a $500 per month budget and the person who has a $20,000 per month budget are in very different situations and are looking for vastly different experiences, campaigns, and levels of expertise from their marketing agency.

At HIVE, we are very clear up front about what the investment looks like to work with us. Sure, we can't give exact numbers (because that is almost impossible, as we'll dive into a bit later), but we give enough information so someone doing their research knows if they can afford us or not.

Many businesses take a custom approach and build service packages around the needs of their customers. And I can just hear them now...

"But Dustin, we don't have exact pricing to share. We don't sell widgets and instead build packages or pricing custom to our customers."

So, you probably have a range of costs, right? You have a general sense of what each project or engagement looks like and have some basic parameters around them? Share that.

This is the world HIVE lives in. We don't have set packages and instead figure out the needs, goals, and budget for our clients so we can build a package that is right for them. But that isn't to say we don't have general guidelines on which to base things. We know, in a general sense, which range each of our services falls into. Of course, there are outliers, but during this phase of research, a general pricing idea is more than adequate for most prospects.

For example, as of March 2023, at HIVE Strategy, we know that our average retainer falls in the $5,000 to $10,000 per month range. We also know that our average website build falls in the $20,000 to $40,000 range. And we know that if you want to run a conversion rate and user experience (CR/UX) campaign with us, you'll be looking at between $6,500 to $12,000 for a four-month sprint.

These figures are by no means exact, but with that information a prospect can come to our website and know if they are the right fit for our agency (at least from a pricing standpoint). If someone comes to our website and is looking to spend $5,000 on a website build, they can easily see that we are probably not the right fit for them. And returning to my earlier example — the organization that has a $500 per month budget for their marketing campaigns can very quickly understand that we don't work with budgets that limited. It's all about transparency and sharing the information that prospects want.

Another excuse I often hear for not sharing pricing information is, "My competitors will find it and undercut us."

So what?

Let's be real here, if your competitors want to find your
pricing, they'll find it. Not much is truly secret anymore
with all the technology we have and all the information
that is readily available online.

I remember early on at HIVE having conversations
with a prospective customer (before we were
transparent with our own pricing) and getting all the
way to the proposal phase. I sent them a proposal and
never heard from them again. I was shocked because
we had such great rapport and very engaging
conversations. I did a little research, and it turned out
the "company" was fake and this person worked for

one of our competitors. She was just trying to get our pricing information and sales processes.

As you can imagine, I was upset at the time. But I realized nothing I gave her was proprietary. We had conversations about her goals and how we could help and I proposed a retainer — that's it. I also decided early on that for my company to succeed, I didn't want to compete solely on price. I don't believe many businesses consistently win by focusing only on price. In fact, always being the cheapest option raises a whole range of issues in the long run.

What's my point? Unless your entire business model is built around being the absolute cheapest option in your industry, your pricing shouldn't be a secret. And even then, if that is your hook, then why would it be a secret?

You're not hurting your competitors by not publishing your pricing. You're hurting the prospects who are researching your company and you're hurting your own sales pipeline.

Put your pricing on your website. Make it easy to find. Being transparent with your pricing, even in generalities or ranges, helps you win more business in the long run.

One of my favorite examples of this is by one of my go-to marketing authors, Marcus Sheridan. Sheridan became a world-renowned speaker after the release of his book, *They Ask You Answer* (a must read, by the way), but his success in the transparent pricing approach didn't begin there. Sheridan was originally an owner of River Pools, a small pool company in Indiana. As he explains in many of his presentations, when the recession hit in 2007, River Pools was on the verge of bankruptcy. Instead of giving in and closing up shop, Sheridan took to inbound marketing to revive his failing business.

One of the main approaches he adopted was business transparency, which meant he answered his audience's questions — especially related to pricing. Many, if not all, of his competitors kept their pricing secret (and still do). Sheridan decided to take the road less traveled and on the River Pools website posted a blog titled, "A Guide to Fiberglass Pool Costs." The post gave a very straightforward breakdown of what customers should expect to spend on a new fiberglass pool, as well as the ongoing costs associated with owning a pool. By providing this information, he became the only business in his industry to provide pricing and this blog post became (and remains) one of River Pool's most popular.

River Pools also rolled out a "Build + Price Your Pool" tool that helps customers go through the entire process of selecting pool options, shows them price ranges along the way, and ends with a form submission to River Pools' sales team.

River Pools, much like HIVE Strategy, doesn't sell one-size-fits-all packages. There is no single or definitive answer to the price of a pool, so they can't publish something that says, "The cost of your pool will be $X." But they *can* still be transparent with their pricing by providing ranges, available options, and the "Build + Price Your Pool" tool.

Sheridan also understood that if his competitors wanted to get his pricing information, they'd get it one way or another. He wasn't going to make the process of finding that information harder for his competitors, just to also make the buying process harder for his customers. He put his customers first. He was transparent. And because of that, River Pools is one of the leaders in their industry and has a huge market share compared to its closest competitors.

Share How the Sausage is Made

I heard something recently that smacked me right in the face…

It's never been easier to start a business, or harder to scale one.

This is so true.

With modern technology, it is very easy to start a business — any kind of business.

I've already written about how little preparation and resources I had when I began HIVE Strategy. Nearly a decade later, I have a very successful agency. It was easy to start the business, but so very hard to scale. It took five years to really figure out how to grow the business in a meaningful and consistent way. We had small, incremental growth each year (with a few outlier years), but over the first five years it was certainly nothing to write home about.

Between 2014 and 2019, we had years of incremental growth followed by small dips. It was a complete rollercoaster until 2020, when we really started to understand who we were, who we weren't, and how to explain that effectively. Since then, we have been on a path of significant growth year over year and project even more growth in 2023.

We currently do about three times the revenue each month than we did in all of 2014. And the main reason is we understand our customers and are transparent with them.

Because it is so easy to start a business, it becomes very difficult to stand out amidst all the noise. I see this every day in the marketing industry. Too often anyone who has a few Instagram followers thinks they're a marketing "guru" and can start a marketing agency.

Oh, how I hate the term "guru." Who actually anoints someone a "guru"? Asking for a friend.

When it comes to differentiation, far too many businesses fall back to, "We provide the best service," or, "We build relationships," instead of sharing how and why they do what they do. There is always the fear of being knocked-off or someone stealing ideas, but pulling the curtain back and sharing more about your story and how you operate can be an amazing trust builder with your audience.

I'm not advising Colonel Sanders to do a commercial for KFC and list the 11 herbs and spices and quantities in their recipes; but I am saying that sharing some behind-the-scenes information (think videos, pictures, and stories) can really humanize a brand. Sharing how KFC sources their chicken, how the staff is trained, how they prepare their chicken, etc., can be extremely insightful and build strong brand authority. It can also immediately answer questions and refute any negative information that may be floating around out there about the brand.

Similarly, Chipotle, the fast casual Mexican restaurant (and potentially the restaurant that takes the most of my money) ran a "For Real" campaign in 2016, which they continue to iterate on today. The campaign highlighted the company's commitment to using real, whole ingredients in their food. It included television ads, social media posts, and in-store signage that emphasized Chipotle's use of real ingredients and its commitment to transparency in their preparation, recipes, and food. The campaign was extremely well received because it shed light on the vast differences between Chipotle's take on creating food and that of its competitors.

How can your brand be more transparent with business operations and processes? How can you give a face to your brand by sharing behind-the-scenes information? The best brands find a way to make their users feel like they are part of the organization and that starts with sharing how the sausage is made.

Answer the Hard Questions

Every industry and business have questions they don't want to answer. Questions they hope are never brought up in the sales process. Questions they would rather run away screaming from than answer.

I get it.

The most frequent question I absolutely hate to hear from a prospect is, "What guarantees do you provide?"

It's easy to understand why a prospect would ask, despite the difficulty I have answering. The problem with guarantees in marketing is there is so much out of our control. As a result, we don't make guarantees because we never want to over-promise and under-deliver. We can't tell a prospect they'll make a specific return on their investment or how many leads they'll generate through our campaigns. And we certainly can't guarantee their campaigns will be huge successes. It just doesn't work that way.

What we can do is give them data on what our other clients have seen and how other campaigns have succeeded. Unfortunately, that doesn't always feel like a great answer to every prospect. It's a difficult question for us to answer and that's why nearly every (good) marketing agency avoids the question. There are not-so-good agencies out there that are happy to provide guarantees, because they are setting the bar very low or doing below board things to ensure they reach those commitments. Examples include purchasing lists of contacts who don't know about your business, spamming links to boost search engine rankings, and purchasing Twitter followers.

And yet, we answered the guarantees question on our website. It was difficult to write, and not an idea everyone in the organization loved, but we did it because it is important to many of our prospective clients.

And as I mentioned before, none of our above-board competitors will come within a hundred feet of that question. This fact alone makes us an authority in the eyes of the prospect, even if our answer may not be what they were hoping or looking for.

Instead of running from those hard questions, tackle them head on. Figure out which questions you (and your industry as a whole) avoid and answer them in a meaningful and public way. You'll be one of the few doing so, and thus will immediately earn the trust and respect of your prospects and customers.

In the late 2010s, the clothing brand Patagonia launched a Fair Trade campaign that turned a common question into an opportunity for introspection for both themselves and customers. The way clothing is made, and the materials used, has become of more interest and concern in recent years, but while many companies work to keep the story of their clothing out of the press, Patagonia asked their customers, "How is your clothing made?" Since Fair Trade factories pay their workers better and have a higher standard of living, the company wanted to highlight that its product was made in this more sustainable way. [3]

The campaign had a two-fold effect: customers began to rethink where they purchased their clothing (which, let's be honest, was from many of Patagonia's competitors) and showcased Patagonia's own practices as a possible path forward for its peers.

Patagonia's campaign took a hard look at not only transparency for their organization, but the industry as a whole. By highlighting the fact that their clothing was made through Fair Trade practices, it also highlighted that others were not managed in the same way. It shed a lot of light on the industry, their practices, and how things could be improved.

Pricing is also an easy one to cite here. So many organizations run from the pricing question or punt to something like, "We need to have a sales conversation or demo first."

Think about some of these questions or scenarios and how you can answer on your website:

- What questions come up regularly throughout your sales process?
- How do you compare (both positively and negatively) to your top competitors?
- Why would someone not purchase from you?

- What other solutions are out there that someone could use to solve their problem, even if it's not with a direct competitor?
- What would you do if you didn't have the budget to afford your company's solution?
- Are there industry regulations do you not comply with or cannot satisfy?
- What customization requests do you not fulfill?

Another option to find potential questions is to do your own research. One of my favorite tools for this is Answer The Public (answerthepublic.com). Neil Patel of NP Digital recently purchased Answer The Public for \$8 million[2] because he saw the importance of understanding the questions people are asking.

Answer The Public does just that. It indexes the most commonly asked questions through Google search queries to give users an idea of what content should be covered, and which questions potential audiences want answered.

To use Answer the Public, you simply input a topic (the recommendation is one or two words for best results), and the tool pulls all the most commonly asked questions around that topic. For example, I ran a search for "HubSpot" and found 387 results and 80 questions. These are the questions my agency should be answering within our content to support people looking for HubSpot solutions and services.

Try it out for yourself and start pulling a list of questions that you can answer for your audience.

It all comes back to transparency. If you're the organization that is willing to answer the tough questions customers are asking, you will build trust and respect from your prospects and will win more business.

This is something Chris Savage, Co-Founder and CEO of Wistia, knows firsthand.

"When someone is using your product, one person might write in and say I have a problem. Nine other people probably have that same problem and never say anything," he said. "If you can take the answer that you had previously given to one person and put

that into your content in a way that now maybe five out

of 10 can see, that's an enormous win."

Activity

Now that we've gone through the Transparency pillar, here are some impactful initial steps that you can take to become more transparent within your marketing campaigns:

1. Make a list of questions your sales team gets in the sales process and create content to answer those (even the difficult or uncomfortable ones).

2. Add pricing information to your website and make it easy to find.

   a. This can be in the form of straight-forward pricing details, a pricing calculator, table, or even just a range of costs.

    b. If you are using a range, be sure to include information about what impacts overall costs.

3. Run a search through Answer the Public (answerthepublic.com) to find questions your audience is asking and create content around those questions. This can be in the form of blog posts, videos, social media posts, website pages, email, and more.

[1] https://spotio.com/blog/sales-statistics/

[2] https://npdigital.com/blog/np-digitals-latest-acquisition-provides-enhanced-customer-insights-for-analytically-driven-marketers/

[3] https://www.forbes.com/sites/bernhardschroeder/2020/01/16/from-the-traditional-to-the-outrageous-four-brands-that-use-honest-transparency-to-build-loyal-customers-with-non-traditional-marketing-and-branding/

CHAPTER THREE

Personality

Who are the people you most like to be around?

Think about that for a second.

Sure, you might answer your spouse or your family or your kids, but outside of that, who are the people you genuinely enjoy spending time with?

The answer is likely the people in your life with the best personalities. They share who they are, connect with you in a unique way, and aren't afraid to be themselves. The same holds true for businesses.

One of the most well-known personality brands is Wendy's, the fast-food chain. Wendy's does a phenomenal job of having a fun and eccentric personality through their social media channels. They are funny, unapologetic, unafraid to push the envelope, and love to spark competition.

If you don't follow Wendy's on Twitter, you're truly missing out; especially if you need the occasional mid-day laugh.

Here are just a couple gems:

You might be saying to yourself, "My business isn't in a fun industry," or, "We sell to a more sophisticated or old school client base that wouldn't appreciate that brash approach to personality."

Those are fair points — you're probably not going to share funny relationship advice or roast someone on social media like Wendy's does if you are in a more conservative industry. But that doesn't mean you can't have personality.

Personality is about more than being funny. It's about finding your voice and making it uniquely your own, in your space. Don't be afraid to go a different direction than your competitors. No one is excited about the same message, language, and vibe coming from every single company in your industry.

Dare to be different and own it. You'll stand out from the crowd and be celebrated for being you.

Dare to be different and own it.

Consider this story, provided by Chris Savage of Wistia. Early in the company's evolution, Wistia's "About Us" page caused a bit of a sensation when they decided to add some personality to the page. Easter eggs were embedded on the page to make it more engaging and fun. By typing "dance" on the page, the employee photos would start switching randomly and music from mash-up master Girl Talk would play.

"The page went viral. It was on the front page of Hacker News and it was on Reddit," Savage said. "I'll never forget that feeling or that moment. This team page has zero to do with our product, but it has people on it. It has personality in it. That was enough to hook people such that they would spend some time with the website, with the brand, trying to figure out what the product was. And we got customers."

Of course, all of this comes with a disclaimer. Being careless, rude, or inappropriate just for the sake of having a personality can easily take things in a negative direction. There is a fine line you must walk as a business between personality and alienating segments of your customer base. Take care with your tone, voice, and personality. If you have an opportunity to show more personality, take it, but understand that there are consequences to going too far or not taking into account how your campaigns may be perceived by your audience.

A striking example of this comes courtesy of the beauty company Dove. The company faced backlash for an advertisement on Facebook that showed a black woman removing her shirt to reveal a white woman. The ad was part of Dove's "Real Beauty" campaign, which was intended to promote self-esteem and body positivity, but that is not how their audience perceived the ad.

Many people interpreted the ad as a message that black skin is dirty or inferior, and that white skin is the "real beauty." While the campaign was not intended to be racist or spark that kind of negativity, the tone, message, and creative did not align with the purpose in the eyes of their audience.[1]

The following recommendations for personality are not one-size-fits-all solutions. Some will work for your brand, maybe even all of them, but the point is to think about how you can add personality to your brand, your messaging, and the interactions you have with your prospects, leads, and customers.

Throughout this chapter, I challenge you to determine what your company's personality currently is and come up with ways you can enhance (or establish) it moving forward. What can you try out? How can you better connect with your prospects? How can you be different than the 100 or 1,000 other companies in your space? What unique characteristics, quirks, and passions do the members of your company have that can shine through in your content?

Note that this isn't going to happen overnight. You can't just determine what your personality is and the next day the whole world understands and associates that personality with your organization. It takes time, effort, and as we'll talk about in a later pillar — consistency. Once you determine what the personality of your company is going to be, you must own it every single day. You must have full buy-in from your team and make a true effort to embrace and share that personality with your audience. This is a long-term play that will pay off, but for you ROI warriors out there, there isn't going to be an immediate return on your efforts. Don't measure it that way — just keep going.

Humor

Humor is one of the best ways to make a connection and this goes for any kind of human interaction. Think about it — how many people have sense of humor at the top of their list when it comes to picking a partner? A huge percentage, because everyone loves laughter and the feelings humor creates.

As organizations, we are largely afraid to have a sense of humor. However, humor is a crucial trait to tap into because it is one of the surest ways to put people at ease, build trust, and encourage connection.

Organizations that let humor contribute to their personality often see a huge boost.

Humor comes in many forms. One of the most reliable forms of humor is sarcasm and "roasting" people, ideas, and companies. It is also one of the riskier approaches and is not for every business. Done well, it can be fun, engaging, and sometimes newsworthy, but if done wrong, it can alienate client bases, sour relationships, and create other catastrophic consequences.

Wendy's does this very well. In the fast-food industry, they use sarcasm and humor to separate themselves from the McDonalds, Taco Bells, and Chick-Fil-As of the world. They banter back and forth with customers (as well as competitors) in a way that is entertaining and clever, but they never cross the line to full-on disrespect.

In fact, Wendy's does this so well it has a dedicated audience all its own. People (myself included) who don't frequent the fast-food chain still engage with and follow it on social media because it has such an entertaining personality. It pushes Wendy's to the front of our minds when thinking about grabbing some fast food, even in a very crowded and competitive space.

Humor doesn't have to be aggressive, especially if that's not your style. Consider ways you can have more fun in your organization or with your prospective customers. Everyone loves to laugh, as we all know.

So, how can you get a laugh out of your audience —
even if it's because of something cheesy. Laughing
builds a bond. Find a way to build that bond with your
audience.

One way we have incorporated humor into HIVE
Strategy is through dad jokes. As a new father, I am a
sincere fan of dad jokes and can't wait until my
daughter is old enough to roll her eyes at my terrible
puns. I have years of dad joke energy saved up for
her. I'm sure to drive her absolutely crazy in her teen
years and I will love every minute of it.

HIVE Strategy first tested out dad jokes through a chat
bot on our website. As we were building out our bot,
we wanted to be different than other agencies out

there with their own bots. The standard chat bot just wasn't going to do it for us, or our audience. We needed something different and unexpected for our website visitors.

One of the options we built into our chat bot was that visitors could choose a "Tell Me a Dad Joke" option, which is by far our most trafficked option. Those jokes are always bee related (to go with the whole HIVE theme, of course) and people love them. We've even had prospects tell us they loved the personality our dad jokes showed. Active prospects commenting on our terrible (and hilarious) dad jokes proved we were on to something and maybe our personality as an agency was fun, energetic, and maybe a little bit corny.

Since then, we've continued the dad joke trend with our monthly newsletters. Each month we have a bee-themed dad joke with our mascot (Buzzy) that is relevant for the time of year. We have done football jokes in August, back to school jokes in September, Christmas jokes during the holidays, and rain jokes in the spring. It's a fun way to engage with our users, even if that engagement is simply a chuckle or eye roll.

We're ok being a little cheesy and fully embrace the idea. It allows us to be a fun agency and clients and prospects notice.

Credit: HIVE Strategy

As we conduct interviews for new roles at our agency, we emphasize to candidates just how critical our culture is. We explain our core values and one of our most important values is fun. I always explain that we aren't in a life-or-death industry. We are in a creative industry that encourages us to have fun, and damnit, we're going to have fun whether it's through corny puns, team time games, or fun Slack channels.

Empathy

Having a personality doesn't have to mean you're funny. It doesn't even have to mean you're overly interesting. Another way to incorporate personality into your marketing is to have empathy for your prospects and customers. Regardless of what your organization does, your prospects have a problem you're trying to solve. Putting yourself in their shoes and understanding what they're going through is vital to building trust.

Every business book in the world reminds readers to understand their customers. This is day one stuff, but you can't run a successful business without this truth. Taking the time to understand your audience instead of treating them as a dollar sign can mean the difference between building trust and growing your business or being viewed as a money-hungry, sleazy company. You must decide what kind of business you want to be.

Empathetic businesses are ones that focus on the needs and concerns of their audience, not just how that audience can spend money with them. They do things that are helpful for their audience, even if it doesn't immediately result in a sale. They create helpful content, consider the pain their audience is dealing with, and even help them find other solutions if their business isn't the right choice. These businesses put their consumers first and realize that by doing so, they will build better and stronger relationships and in the long run will create new business. Sometimes that just isn't an immediate sale, and as empathetic organizations, they should be fine with that.

Empathy isn't only about understanding what your audience is going through, but also accounting for the things they may be privately experiencing.

One recent example I came across was a marketing campaign for expectant mothers. The campaign had good intentions (as nearly all campaigns do), but it failed to have empathy for the fact that unfortunately not all expectant mothers have happy births. In this campaign, the company did a great job creating messaging that resonated with mothers and celebrated the new life about to come into the world. But it didn't consider that around 10-20% of pregnancies end in miscarriage[2].

The company relied heavily on marketing automation to send out their messages, and after around ten months, it sent a message congratulating the mother on their new arrival. For the majority who had successful, healthy births, it worked out well. But what do you think the reaction was from the mothers and families who had miscarriages or complications with their birth? It's a safe bet that receiving those messages was extremely traumatizing and painful.

The company was trying to share in the joy of a new life, but this was a situation where it leaned too much into their tools and marketing automation and potentially alienated a segment of its audience in an extremely unpleasant way.

To be successful in marketing today, we need to have great processes, solid messaging, utilize technology and marketing automation, and truly understand what our audience may be going through or looking for.

Relying too heavily on technology can cause major issues with personalization, engagement, and in the very worst cases, extreme audience alienation.

Before you launch that marketing automation campaign, think about all the cases involved and how it will be received by your audience. What would you think if you received your messaging? Would you engage with it, or would it feel like it came from a soulless organization?

Empathy can be a real tool and asset for your company, or potentially a real problem. You need to choose, and you should do the work and take extra steps to empathize with your prospects, leads, and customers. Don't short cut this or eventually you'll pay for it.

Competition

We all have competition. Regardless of what you tell yourself or how you view your organization, you have competition. Believe me, in my nearly 10 years of running HIVE, more than a few clients have told me how unique they are and how they have no competition. They're unicorns.

Every single time I roll my eyes (even if it's just in my mind).

There's a slim chance you have some technology or process that's truly unique to your organization. Maybe you don't have a direct competitor from that standpoint, but every purchasing decision is just that

— a decision. The consumer is choosing between working with you or another organization. Or maybe they're choosing between your organization or a completely different solution in a different industry. Indirect competitors are still competitors you need to take into account. In some situations, your consumer might choose between working with you or to doing nothing at all. Indecision is also a competitor.

Now, how does this fit with personality?

There are many ways you can incorporate competition into your messaging, content, and personality.

The first is to go directly after your closest competitors. This is something Wendy's does well — it isn't shy to

call out how it is better than McDonalds, Burger King,
or In-N-Out Burger (amongst others — truly, no one is
safe). It takes shots at their competitors' marketing
campaigns and products through clever puns and
jokes to promote its proclaimed superior product.

This approach also works for more indirect
competitors.

I saw a great local example of this recently while I was in line at Chick-Fil-A. I was in the seemingly mile-long drive thru line, getting annoyed with how long the wait was, and I looked across the parking lot to see a huge banner hung on a TGI Fridays restaurant in the same parking lot that said, "Why Cluck Around In The Drive-Thru?" I was blown away by the creativity, humor, and use of a somewhat indirect competition angle to connect with the people who were struggling with the long line at the fast-food restaurant.

TGI Fridays did a great job of understanding that people in line for Chick-Fil-A were probably all tired of waiting in line and reminded them they didn't need to wait in that line. Honestly, I never paid much attention to TGI Fridays. Now I am very aware it's there and it immediately joined the list of restaurants I'll consider when my wife and I go out for dinner.

TGI Fridays isn't a direct competitor to Chick-Fil-A. It's a sit-down restaurant where customers go to have a drink, play some games, and be served by staff. Chick-Fil-A is a chicken fast food restaurant that is famous for their chicken sandwiches and waffle fries. They're vastly different restaurants, but at the same time, you're not going to choose both for dinner. Even though neither restaurant would list the others as a competitor, proximity makes them one in this case.

And finally, remember that your consumers always have the option to do nothing. That is a real competitor for every business in the world. Incorporating

messaging to help consumers understand the impact

and cost of indecision can also be important to your

personality.

Activity

Now that we've gone through the Personality pillar, here are some impactful initial steps you can take to add more personality to your marketing campaigns:

1. Talk to your team (including everyone from executives to interns) to better understand their personalities. Incorporating your team's personality into your campaigns will make the content feel more authentic and impactful.

2. Take stock of the content you have produced in the past and review for personality. What is the tone and theme of this content? Did it resonate with your target audience? Could you

incorporate more personality into a revision of this content?

3. Review your competitors' personalities. How can you stand out in comparison by incorporating more (or a different) personality?

[1] https://www.latrobe.edu.au/news/articles/2017/opinion/dove-real-beauty-and-the-racist-history

[2] https://www.mayoclinic.org/diseases-conditions/pregnancy-loss-miscarriage/symptoms-causes/syc-20354298

CHAPTER FOUR

Authenticity

We live in a world where those who aren't authentic are left behind or ignored. Modern consumers can smell inauthenticity a mile away — the last thing you want is to be compared to a used car salesman who is only trying to force a sale and doesn't care about their customer's needs.

Today, being authentic means much more than just not pushing a hard sell on someone. It means following through on your promises every single time, being who you are and not pretending to be something you're not, involving yourself in social causes that matter to your organization, and even being willing to fail and make mistakes. Consumers understand we aren't perfect. And businesses that are willing to try and possibly fail are, believe it or not, applauded for their authenticity and willingness to make honest mistakes. It makes your organization relatable and human.

As you think about what it means to be authentic, it's important to embrace your brand's uniqueness and not conform to what you *think* your audience or society wants you to be.

How do you go about projecting an authentic brand to your audience? It doesn't happen quickly. It takes effort — and not a one-time, big push kind of effort.

Think instead about a consistent, every day for years and years kind of effort. That's what it takes to create a truly authentic brand to which consumers relate.

If you were looking for a quick answer or an easy trick to become a more authentic brand, that probably wasn't the answer you were hoping for. But the process of becoming an authentic brand can start today and can become part of how you discuss your brand, engage with your prospects, leads, and customers, and can be incorporated into your marketing collateral moving forward.

Ready? Let's dive in.

Follow Through on Your Promises

One non-negotiable feature that applies to your brand and how you engage with prospects, leads, and customers is follow through.

You cannot be an authentic brand if you don't follow-through on your promises.

Through marketing campaigns, messaging, engagement with prospects, and even brand presentation; all companies make promises. Whether they are explicitly stated or assumed by the audience, businesses are making promises through their marketing. And the follow-through on these promises drastically impacts both brand and audience perception.

While HIVE may not explicitly guarantee specific results (there are far too many variables to say, "We guarantee your marketing campaigns with HIVE will result in $X million dollars in new revenue"), our clients assume that as a successful and reputable marketing agency, we are going to follow through on the deliverables and strategy needed to reach those revenue goals. Our promise, while not explicitly stated in our marketing campaigns or collateral, is to succeed for our clients and grow their businesses.

Whether you are making flat-out promises and guarantees or not in your messaging, you are making commitments to your audience. Your consumers are very aware of your commitments and are watching to see how you follow through.

It can cost you if you don't keep your commitments, as this FedEx example demonstrates. For customers who use services like FedEx First Overnight and Standard Overnight, customers can request their money back if the package isn't delivered by the promised time. Not only does failing take money away from FedEx, it also really crushes brand loyalty — why would a customer return to a company that can't meet their expected delivery time?

Don't be the sleazy used car salesman that promises the world and then lets your customers drive off in a lemon. The follow-through is even more important than the message in your marketing campaign.

Be Who You Are

We all want to be liked and remembered, but far too often businesses try to be something they are not because they *think* that is what their audience wants them to be. Trying to fit a perceived mold or model of what you think the world wants is a sure way to fail. The businesses that are truly perceived as authentic are those that own what and who they are, faults and all.

That means whatever the personality of your business is, own it. Embrace it. Love it. You don't have to be the cool brand everyone wants to emulate. You don't have to be the funny brand people follow for a laugh. And you don't have to be the stuffy brand you think everyone in your industry expects you to be.

If you're funny — be funny.

If you're clever — be clever.

If you're straight-edge — be straight-edge.

If you're focused on activism — share your passions and the causes closest to your heart.

If you're pushing an agenda — push it (but don't try to cover it up).

You don't have to fit a mold.

You don't have to play a part, regardless of the industry or business you're in. You can be authentically you. Law firms don't have to be uptight and rigid. Medical clinics can have a sense of humor. And your real estate company can drop a tasteful f-bomb here and there (if it's who you are and who you want to be).

Be you and your audience will follow.

One of my favorite examples of this came from Kraft. Kraft is famous for its macaroni and cheese, with mothers and children as an obvious audience. It has built an entire business on Kraft Mac & Cheese (though they do have a very large catalog of other products). In 2017, Kraft decided to add some humor to their campaign targeting mothers.

For Mother's Day they ran a "Swear Like A Mother" campaign[1], embracing the imperfection of mothers and the fact that 74% of parents say they've sworn in front of their kids.

In the hilarious ads, Kraft created a variety of comical swear word replacements and sensors using macaroni noodles. The brand recruited Melissa Mohr, Ph.D., and author of *Holy Sh*t*, to be the spokesperson for the campaign. In the ads, Mohr shares a day in the life of a mother of three crazy kids who run around the house, fail to listen, and even leave their Legos out to be stepped on.

The ad is extremely relatable to parents (regardless of their kids' ages) and shares the comical side of the daily frustrations of being a mother. To further enhance the campaign, the company rolled out fun boxes of Kraft Mac & Cheese shaped like Mother's Day cards, and even included a pair of "Fail-Cancelling Ear Plugs." Shaped like macaroni noodles, of course.

Through this campaign, not only did Kraft do a great job appealing to their main audience (mothers), but it also exemplifies several pillars of marketing like a human. Kraft used its personality to share humor and the imperfections of being a mother. The company was also unapologetically itself. Kraft is not a stuffy brand. It's fun and creates products families, mothers, and children love. And it made quite the social campaign and impact.

Credit: Kraft

Social Responsibility

We live in a world that values social responsibility and brands that take up a cause, support it, and share that cause with their audience are winning and will continue to win.

We're talking about authenticity here, so I am not advising you to take up a cause to sell more products or services. I am, however, saying that as organizations, we all have a responsibility to make the world a better place. We have resources. We have an audience. And we have a stage. We need to use that stage to champion issues that we care about to improve our world.

In fact, according to HubSpot, 45% of businesses are focused on increasing their social responsibility over the next year[2].

Consumers gravitate towards businesses that care about more than just a sale. They gravitate towards businesses that stand for something; businesses that believe in something.

Businesses that care.

Of course, this is not your marketing campaign alone (other individuals and organizations are also supporters), but it does confirm an authentic business image that is part of a community (even if it is a global community). We'll dive more into community in a later pillar.

Your cause can be anything you're passionate about. A great place to start is to take an interest in the specific passions of your team, clients, and families. At HIVE, we have championed several causes over the years, ranging from feeding children at underprivileged schools in the Denver metro area and school supply drives to other causes such as startup business events and supporting women's career growth. These are all issues our team cares deeply about and we were thrilled to support them.

Businesses today can't just be about revenue and profit. If they're going to grow, build a loyal audience, and continue to have an impact with marketing and sales initiatives — they must care about more than dollars. They must care about something deeper.

Find your organization's passions and invest in them.

Go Live

Going live had a huge surge when the option first popped up on social media platforms. Everyone wanted to go live for anything and everything.

Honestly, it was a bit chaotic. I remember getting notifications that so-and-so was going live, only to join the session to see the top of their forehead while they tried to figure out how to do it right. It was a weird time, to say the least.

Fast forward several years and going live has died off considerably. Individuals and businesses are nervous and afraid to go live because it introduces an element of imperfection. There is the opportunity to mess up. You might stumble over your words, mispronounce something, or — *gasp* — you might even lose your train of thought for a second.

I don't mean to down-play this or mock those insecurities. They are legitimate fears. After all, there's a reason public speaking is the top fear in the world. It's intimidating and can be quite scary. But as an organization, if you want to grow your audience, brand recognition, and ultimately your business, you have to be willing to fail. You have to be willing to be human. You have to be ok with the fact that you're not always going to be perfect.

Here's the kicker — people actually respect it.

People empathize with the imperfect. There is literally no movie out there where the protagonist is perfect. They all have imperfections and that's what makes them relatable and worth caring about. Messing up or having a bad day is part of the human experience. Businesses that pretend to always be perfect, only say the exact right thing, and only do the expected, aren't memorable. They're not relatable. They're not authentic, since we all know that even if they project a perfect picture, they're not perfect in reality.

Nordstrom's Facebook Live campaign[3] was a particularly risky live campaign, but one that worked extremely well. Nordstrom launched a live video campaign called "Live from the Sales Floor," in which the company used Facebook Live to stream video from its stores. The videos featured employees showcasing products and interacting with viewers in real-time. There was plenty of opportunity for mistakes, and without a script, some happened, but it was also extremely entertaining and relatable for their audience. The campaign was successful in driving traffic to the Nordstrom website and increasing sales.

Going live doesn't have to be the medium you choose (though it can be very impactful, as currently there is far less competition and social networks want you to use that tool), but the point is that taking a chance and failing (even publicly) will build a lot of trust with your audience. It will show your human side. We can all relate to a misstep here and there. Life isn't scripted.

Take the chance — no outcome is worse than doing nothing.

Activity

Now that we've gone through the Authenticity pillar, here are some impactful initial steps you can take to become more authentic within your marketing campaigns:

1. Review your content for any explicit or implicit promises and ensure you have a plan to follow through on those promises. It's always better to under promise and over deliver than the other way around.

2. Eliminate any barriers or constraints you have around your industry or your business. You don't have to fit a mold. Determine who you

are and who you want to be as a company and
own it.

3. Share the causes you believe in, as well as
how you are supporting them and how others
can get involved. Even if your causes aren't
directly related to your organization, share
them with your audience. It will make your
organization feel more human and will build an
immense amount of trust.

   a. If there aren't any social causes that
   you currently support, do some
   research and see how your
   organization can get involved in your
   community. It doesn't need to be
   monetary involvement. Encourage your
   team to volunteer, spread the word, or

even do some pro bono work. There
are many ways to get involved in your
community.

4. If you have someone at your organization who
    is comfortable on camera, make a plan to go
    live at least once per month on the social
    networks that make sense for your target
    audience. Most social media platforms today
    offer some version of live streaming for users
    and businesses.

5. Share real customer stories in your marketing
    campaigns. No one likes to be first when it
    comes to working with an organization.
    Prospects want to know that others have done
    it and succeeded. Share social proof and case

studies to help your campaigns and company to feel more genuine and relatable.

6. Review all your content for language and voice. If your messaging is overly salesy, rewrite it to be more helpful and authentic. Use your own voice and language to better connect with your audience.

7. Your mission and vision should be at the heart of all your decisions. Straying away from these core values can make your company feel inauthentic and disingenuous. Review every decision, campaign, and piece of content through the lens of your organization's mission and vision statements.

[1] https://www.youtube.com/watch?v=sgBVrEb_qXY

[2] https://blog.hubspot.com/marketing/hubspot-blog-marketing-industry-trends-report

[3] https://www.retaildive.com/news/nordstrom-debuts-interactive-livestreams/596869/

CHAPTER FIVE

Consistency

When it comes to marketing, few things can kill your momentum as quickly as poor consistency. Consistency in brand, consistency in content, and consistency in message. To succeed in today's hyper-competitive landscape, you need to show up and show up well every time.

This book is about how we can humanize our brand and be better marketers by treating our audience like the humans they are. Consistency in how brands show up is paramount to this overall goal. Ask yourself:

- Are we confusing our audience?

- Are we keeping our brand intact?

- Are we sharing the same type of messaging?

- And most importantly, are we showing up when, where, and how we're expected to show up?

The famous saying, "Showing up is half the battle" is never more applicable than it is to marketing. To be great, businesses must be seen. Our message must be seen. Our brand must be seen. And to be seen, we simply must show up and show up consistently. That's how we become memorable and that's how we win.

Consistency in Brand

There is a reason successful brands are particular about how their brand is used, portrayed, and represented. They manage everything about their brand down to the smallest detail because every step tells a story. Your brand is what you make it and how your audience will perceive it. If it's all over the place or inconsistent, your brand will be viewed as unorganized, confusing and forgettable.

So, how do you maintain a consistent brand?

It begins with brand guidelines. You need to take every circumstance into account and manage how your brand is used, especially if it's used outside of your owned media (your website or social media accounts). Let's examine the brand visual elements you need to manage. Then we will explore the language and communication elements of your brand.

Visual Brand Elements

Logo

- Where will your logo be used?

- How will your logo be used?

- Are there different variations of your logo?

- Can the logo be altered to become an icon?

- Will the color of your logo change when placed over different backgrounds?

- Can the logo be placed over textured backgrounds?

- Can the logo be stretched, manipulated, or altered in any way?

Your logo *is* your brand and keeping very tight regulations around its use, both internally and externally, is vitally important. Your organization should outline every scenario that could arise so there is no issue with the appearance or perception of your brand in public.

While it may feel like overkill to outline every detail of your logo usage, the fact is, if you give someone an inch, they'll take a mile. And you definitely don't want anyone taking a mile's worth of leeway with your logo.

Colors

- What is your primary color palette?

  Colors are very important for your brand. Think about it — what colors do you associate with McDonald's? Red and gold, obviously. What about Best Buy? Blue and yellow. How about more business-to-business brands like HubSpot? Orange. Salesforce? Sky blue. And what about Adobe? Red.

  Regardless of what your business does or sells, color can be a defining trait that helps consumers associate your brand with what you do.

  It is important to share information in all color

formats so there is never any question about what the color is for each format. This includes RGB (for web), CMYK (for print), and HEX codes.

Additionally, you should outline which colors in your palette are your primary colors and which are secondary. You may have colors used only in certain circumstances or as highlight colors. You may also have background colors or general light and dark colors that shouldn't be used as your brand's primary colors.

- How can your colors be used?
  There are likely colors in your palette that don't look great on top of or next to each other, and

even present accessibility issues if they are used in specific ways.

Again, being as specific as possible will save your brand from an unfortunate design or layout that looks bad or isn't accessible to certain populations.

Typography

- What are your primary fonts and font sizes? In this section, you should be thinking about written content. How do you want it to appear? Think about your headings — will your H1 (primary heading), H2 (secondary heading), H3, H4, H5, H6, and paragraph text have font specifications associated with them? Most brands have at least two fonts — one for headings and one for paragraph fonts.

Heading fonts are typically bolder and more eye-catching than paragraph fonts. The idea is there will be fewer words using these fonts, but they will be impactful words that draw your audience in.

Paragraph font, in contrast, should be legible and not fatigue your reader's eyes. For paragraph fonts, the simpler the better. I am very much on team sans-serif (no extending features like the font of this page) over a serif font like Georgia.

The difference in ease of reading is substantial, especially if there's a lot of text.

Imagery

- What type of imagery will you use and in which circumstances?

- Will your brand be using graphical imagery or photography?

- If you're using photography, will you allow stock photography, or will it all be owned and/or created media?

- If you're going with graphical imagery, will you use a flat or 3D style?

- If you're using photography, will you be incorporating people, products, landscapes, and other elements?

- What are the demographics of the people in your images?

- What subset of the population are you attempting to highlight?

- What level of diversity is important?

- What characteristics do they need to have?

- How will they be positioned?

Your imagery speaks to who your brand is and should be consistent with the other elements of your brand. It should speak to your purpose, messaging, your color palette, etc.

There is a lot to consider when it comes to including people in your imagery. As a good rule of thumb, people in your images should directly relate to your target audience. They should be representations of your best customers and the people you work best with.

Another tip to get the most out of your imagery is to ensure the people are always looking in the direction of the most important content. It's human nature to follow the eyes of a subject, so if they're looking towards your form or a key piece of information, your audience will naturally look that direction more frequently.

Again, this all returns to consistency. Your images and the people in them should be consistent. They should have a consistent theme. They should be geared toward a consistent audience.

Consistency in Content

The previous section included many details and tactics intentionally. Next, we can move on to content. And while we all know more content is better, not all content is useful and simply creating content for the sake of creating content doesn't do anyone any good.

From this perspective, it's important to have a firm grasp on the purpose of your content. Is it educational? Is it sales driven? Is it for entertainment?

Regardless of its purpose, your content should exist for a reason and if any content — I mean ANY content, regardless of how long you spent on it or how much you have invested in it — isn't consistent with the work your company does, then it needs to be scrapped or, at the very least, reevaluated.

Think about it — what would you think if *The Onion*, the satirical publication, suddenly published an in-depth, hard-hitting article on homelessness in America. You'd be super confused, as would every single one of their readers. Or if HubSpot suddenly started sharing content on their social networks about what's happening in the cryptocurrency world. It doesn't fit with what their content is meant to be. *The Onion* is known for satire, so publishing research-heavy, investigative journalism doesn't fit with what their audience expects. HubSpot focuses on education-based content around the world of marketing and sales, not financial news.

While these examples may seem obvious, this can also happen more subtly: perhaps the way you address your audience or the types of products you feature suddenly change. People will notice. Be aware of your content, who it's for, and why they care. Creating content just because you need to publish new content can create more issues than it solves.

Consistency in Messaging

Consistency in messaging goes hand-in-hand with consistency in content, but messaging focuses on your tone, voice, and topics. How are you portraying your message across your outlets?

Keep a consistent tone and voice in all messaging, from blog posts and videos to emails and social media posts. It matters. People pay attention to messaging and will notice if something is off. More than that, consistent messaging establishes your brand and makes it more recognizable.

By consistently focusing on messaging and incorporating the other pillars I've discussed, you can start to create a tone, voice, and message all your own. This strengthens the rapport with your audience and confirms your position as a reliable and trusted voice in your industry.

Nothing Happens Overnight

Finally, it's important to think about consistency in content creation. Content creation, and marketing in general, is not meant for the faint of heart. It's hard work and will always be a challenge. It means creating content calendars, schedules, drafts, outlines, and tasks to make sure that when your audience expects a new video to be released at 11 a.m. each Tuesday, that it's released every Tuesday at exactly 11 a.m.

We're all creatures of habit. I know every Monday morning I am going to receive an email from HubSpot, I'm going to see a reel from my favorite influencer on Facebook every day at lunch, and on the first of each month I'm going to receive an RSS email from HIVE

Strategy with all the blog content we published last month. Consistency in creation is important to your audience and the more reliable you can become with your content, the faster it will grow.

Being predictable is a vastly underrated skill in marketing. Just show up when people are expecting you and you'll be 50% further along than almost any other business.

Being predictable is a vastly underrated skill in marketing.

Additionally, search engines appreciate it. It's widely accepted that consistent content is more likely to rank higher in search engine results pages, and that's because it's reliable. When Google knows you publish a blog post every day at 8:15 a.m., the algorithms can expect it. When you post sporadically and inconsistently, the spiders aren't looking for your new content.

Activity

Now that we've gone through the Consistency pillar, here are some impactful initial steps you can take to become more consistent within your marketing campaigns:

1. Create a brand guide and stick to it. Your brand is everything and needs to be protected. You can start a brand guide by using tools like Brand Folder (brandfolder.com), Brandtools (brand.tools), and even Canva (canva.com), among many others. It's important to have a documented brand guide that is shared throughout your organization, so that everyone is using your brand in an appropriate way.

2. Use real photos and videos wherever possible. Using real photos and videos in your campaigns, rather than stock images or staged footage makes your campaigns feel more authentic, genuine, and consistent.

3. Create a content calendar and stick to it. As you create your calendar, think about what stage of the buyer's journey your audience is in, which of your target personas care most about each piece of content, your audience's preferred medium for receiving and engaging with your work, and what the next step in their journey will be.

4. Recruit help. Many organizations lack the necessary resources to get content created and published and often it falls on one person,

which is just a recipe for disaster. Recruit help from within your organization or tap into outside resources to ensure you stick to your content plan and deliver the consistent content search engines and audiences crave.

CHAPTER SIX

Helpful

Do people who answer questions with a question bug you? Yeah, me too.

In a way, asking a question is an act of vulnerability — you're admitting there's something you don't know. It can be easier for some and more difficult for others, but regardless of how you feel when asking a question, we can all agree that responding helpfully to any query earns you a positive response from the asker.

With that in mind, why not become *the* resource for your clients when they have questions? Being the place customers know they can go to when they're wondering about your industry, product, service, or solution will not only build positive connections between visitors and your company, but also gives you the opportunity to get your content in front of them at the same time.

As I covered earlier in this book, we as organizations are no longer in control. We don't control when someone comes to us with a question or to discuss a potential sale. Our prospects are now empowered to do their own research, find answers to their own questions, and determine (without the help of a salesperson) which solution is best for them. This pillar is all about how organizations can be more human in their approach to content by being more helpful and by placing their full emphasis and focus on being a resource to their audience.

To be most helpful, everything should be driven by the audience — including prospects, leads, and even current and past customers.

We need to understand the questions our audience is asking, what they're looking for, the information they need to make an accurate assessment of their problem and potential solutions, and we need to do it all (and this can't be hammered home enough) without reverting back to our advertising roots and hitting them with a sales pitch with every piece of content.

Our audiences are not looking to be sold. They're looking to be helped. They have a problem, and they are looking for information to make the right decision about the solution and who provides it. There is a time and a place for a sales pitch, but that place is not in your educational content.

Check yourself when writing your content. Are you coming off too salesy? Are you pushing your audience to a next step in the journey that does not align with where the reader or viewer may be in their process? Does the next step align with the goals of the person engaging with your content?

To be as helpful as possible to your audience, first you must take a step back and truly understand who you're talking to and how they want to consume your content.

Understanding your audience and their place in the buyer's journey is the most important step in creating helpful content.

You can't be helpful in your marketing or in your content without having a crystal-clear picture of who that content is intended for. The content in this phase that most often falls flat is too general or tries to support too many audiences. Before you even start any of your educational content, ask yourself who it is intended for and who would most benefit from it. If the answer is too general or broad, it might be time to rethink that topic or idea.

Your helpful and education-focused content should be centered on specific topics for specific audiences. It should be intended to address specific questions, issues, and concerns that someone has with their problem, the solutions available to them, or the companies, products, or services they are considering. Each of these areas ties directly back to the stages of the buyer's journey.

Many of you may be intimately familiar with the stages of the buyer's journey, but let's do a quick refresher on the stages:

Awareness Stage

This stage of the buyer's journey is where a prospect realizes they have a problem. They may not be able to identify the problem, but they are starting to learn about the causes and issues behind it. In this stage, your audience is looking for helpful information on what is happening to them and why.

In the awareness stage, your audience is interested in content that helps them to identify and put a name to their problem.

As an example, at HIVE Strategy we get a lot of awareness stage traffic around conversion rate optimization. The prospect likely doesn't even know what that term means, but they are looking for information on why more of their website traffic isn't converting into leads. They are usually also concerned with click through rates (the percentage of people who take a next step or click on a call-to-action), views of landing pages, and user experience and interface issues.

In this stage of the journey, we create social media posts, white papers, eBooks, blog posts, website copy, and videos that explain what conversion rate optimization and user experience design are. We combined these two concepts into CR/UX (conversion rate and user experience), a specialty service offering at HIVE. We also answer questions around converting more leads, improving time on page, decreasing bounce rate, and design issues that can cause visitors to disengage with a website.

Consideration Stage

Moving on to the consideration stage, we are looking at content for an audience that has clearly defined what their problem is and given it a name. This audience is researching to fully understand the solutions at their disposal, which could include purchasing a product or service, consulting, training, process change, or even doing nothing at all. The audience at this stage is solely focused on understanding what options are available to them and how they would fit into their processes.

As a marketer, it's important to answer questions and compare the different options to give your audience all the information they need to make the right decision for their situation.

Continuing our example from earlier, once our audience has a strong understanding that their problem lies in not being able to convert traffic on their website due to user experience and conversion rate optimization issues, they are then looking for ways to remedy the issue. They are going to need content and education around HIVE's CR/UX campaign, as well as learning how to run conversion rate optimization themselves. Additionally, they will need to understand tools like Hotjar and Lucky Orange to collect data, how to go about getting a new website design, A/B testing, and how each of those options impacts their business.

For this stage of the buyer's journey, we might create white papers, eBooks, blog posts, website copy, webinars, podcasts, and videos that explain how each of those options works, how they compare to each other, the costs associated with each, and how effective they can be in converting leads, increasing time on page, and decreasing bounce rate.

Note that we still haven't asked for a sale. Or a conversation with a salesperson. In these first two stages, it's not about you. It's about your audience and educating them. Wait your turn!

Decision Stage

Finally, after all that work, we have reached the stage everyone wants to jump to immediately. It's time to sell and help your audience understand why they should work with your organization instead of one of your competitors.

At this stage of the buyer's journey, your audience has determined that they have a problem, given their problem a name, researched potential solutions, and identified the right solution for them. Now they need to determine who they will work with on that solution.

This is not where you should gate everything (putting your content behind a form) or push every interaction to buy; but it is an opportunity to share more about your company, your solutions, how you've helped others with the same problem, and offer a sales, coaching, or an introductory meeting.

Returning to the earlier example, if a prospect decides they need a conversion rate optimization and user experience campaign, now they are deciding between HIVE Strategy and other marketing agencies out there that provide these services. After all, there are plenty of agencies that perform CRO and UX design. Now, it is my obligation as a marketer to share details about why we are the right choice and how we're different from those other agencies.

For this stage of the buyer's journey, we create case studies, authority pieces, speaking engagements, deep dive content, blog posts, website copy, comparison charts, webinars, podcasts, and videos explaining HIVE's expertise — how we're different, what it's like to work with us, expectations, successes, certifications, and more. This is an opportunity to educate and still be helpful, but now the topic is our company. We are educating prospects about us and why they should work with us. It's just a different spin on being helpful with our content.

The problem is most marketers and salespeople want to immediately jump to this stage. They create a lot of content for this stage because they like to tell the world about how great they are. However, most of their audience will never reach this stage because they never took the time to engage them in the first two stages.

Taking your time to understand where someone is in this process and meeting them where they are with your content can mean the difference between a closed deal and a person who never returns to your website.

Thanks for embarking on that journey with me (pun totally intended). Now that we've covered what the buyer's journey is, let's meet our prospects (or who they should be).

Your Audience

Understanding our audience is far more than determining a target audience or even singular target persona. Over the course of my career, I have often talked about personas and why they're necessary. I still think personas are extremely valuable, but I also believe that we, as marketers, need to take that concept significantly further.

Personas, as defined by HubSpot, are fictional, generalized characters that encompass the needs, goals, and behavior patterns of your customers. In other words, they're your target customers and who you want to work with. This should be informed by past data, interviews and research into your best customers, and a sales and marketing combined effort to determine who these people are, what they look like, and what they care about.

We have a tool at HIVE Strategy that helps us create the ideal target personas (yes, always plural) for our clients, but what we've seen is most organizations don't put the right level of effort into this process.

Your personas should be the guide for all your marketing, not just a general idea of who you want to work with. This means truly taking the time to accurately research, interview, and engage with your audience to build out these profiles. You need to understand who they are, what makes them tick, where they live, what they struggle with, and how to help them. Each persona is going to be vastly different because they all have different needs, goals, and problems you can help solve. Taking the time to build these profiles out and update them regularly (at least every six months) will help you generate more helpful content because you will have a much firmer grasp on who you're creating your content for and how it helps them.

Here is an example of a target persona. Feel free to use these prompts as a starting point for building out your own personas, but don't stop there. Think about how you can help this person, what content you can create for them in the awareness, consideration, and decision stages, and how to best engage with them.

Restaurant Owner Owen

AGE	40's	EDUCATION	Prestigious Culinary School
TITLE	Restaurant Owner & Chef	CERTIFICATES	N/A
LOCATION	Chicago, Illinois	DIRECT REPORTS	Operations Manager
SALARY	$180,000	REPORTS TO	None

Innovative Data-driven Team Player

Restaurant Owner Owen

GOALS

- Want to make a smart decision about markets for expansion
- Looking for market research about where customers are spending money and time
- Looking to improve buying and distributing along supply chain for multiple sites
- Needs support in determining financial benchmarks and readiness for expansion

FRUSTRATIONS

- Frustrated by the highly competitive restaurant industry and ensuring that their concept succeeds
- Frustrated by the lack of data to help them make decisions about expansion, supply, and demand
- Challenged to maintain high-quality dining experience while budgeting and turning a profit

BIO

Owen is a high-end restaurant owner who attended a prestigious culinary institute before traveling around the world as a chef and food connoisseur. Owen returned to Chicago ten years ago to open his first restaurant and has opened two more since. He aims to bring the innovative culinary inspiration from his world travels back home. His concept offers guests a high-end dining experience that has proven to be very successful. He is interested in growth and expanding his restaurant business, and he is looking for the right support to make it happen.

Creating Content for All Stages of the Buyer's Journey

Once you have a clear understanding of who your audience is and what their problems are, and reeducated yourself on the buyer's journey stages, it's time to really think about the content in those stages.

It can be very easy to jump right to the decision stage and produce a lot of sales-focused content, but that is why most marketing campaigns fall flat. They're only focused on making that sale, not being helpful.

Having a truly impactful and helpful campaign requires a variety of content in each stage; content that meets your prospects at the right stage in their journey. And be sure not to leave out the first two stages. Take the time to map out helpful content that speaks to the questions and pain points your audience is having in each stage. By doing this, you will see a significantly higher percentage of your audience move from one stage to the next.

Now is the time to go back to that more than 50 pieces of content per month that we talked about in The Problem chapter and start to divvy it up between the stages (while focusing on areas where you are currently weakest).

Creating Helpful Content

Now that we know who we are creating content for and how to use it to reach our audience in each stage of the buyer's journey, it's time to create the helpful content.

Despite how often I've used the term "helpful content," you might still be wondering what it is. Simply put, it's educational content that helps a user in their research process as they search for a solution to a problem.

Helpful content can take many formats and lengths and can be shared through a variety of mediums.

Potential formats can include any or all the following (and are not limited to just these):

- Website pages and copy
- Blog posts
- Videos and video series
- Podcasts and individual episodes
- Social media posts
- Landing pages

- Emails

- Events

- Webinars

- Interviews

- Books

- Speaking engagements

- Print

- Radio

- Television and OTT

- Press and media

- Downloadable content like eBooks, white papers, infographics, checklists, etc.

With each of these different formats, the length and level of depth will vary greatly. Obviously, you can't be as detailed in a tweet as you can with a downloadable eBook or five-minute video. Don't feel like you must solve every problem with every piece of content. The point is to provide value in supporting the education of your audience. This can be surface level or down to the core.

To create successful content, think about how your audience wants to consume your work. Do they prefer brief content they can digest in small chunks? Or would they prefer very in-depth material that dives deep on a topic? What is their preference on written content, audio, video, or some combination?

As a best practice, you should test out content of different lengths, level of expertise, and format to determine what resonates best with your audience. As you collect data, you'll be able to make more sophisticated decisions about length, format, and depth of topic moving forward.

Get Your Content in Front of Your Audience

Once you have determined the content you're creating, for whom, in what format, and in which stage of the funnel, you're still not quite done.

Great, helpful content is really only impactful if it can be found. So much useful work goes to the content graveyard early simply because no one knows it exists.

As a marketer, it can be easy to say our audience doesn't care about a topic or a format doesn't work because no one is engaging with it, but first you need to take a step back and determine if the issue really lies in the fact that your audience can't find it.

Unfortunately, this isn't the Field of Dreams. Just because you create great content, doesn't mean that people are automatically going to flock to it. This is where great marketing campaigns come into play.

Promotion of your helpful content can come in many forms, but the first step should be to make sure that it is optimized for search. Ensure that your content is keyword focused, included in your sitemaps, and submitted to search engines. Then be sure to share your new resources with other websites, companies, industry experts, and blogs that may want to link to it. The more links you can get to your resources, the more likely it is to be found through search. This book is not about search engine optimization tips or tactics, but taking the time to ensure your content ranks and is found though search should be the first step in your promotion process.

Next, think about incorporating content into your different campaigns. Sharing new content through email, social, advertising, in your blog, through guest posts, influencers, and other portions of your marketing strategy is critical.

For your content to truly be helpful, it must get in front of the people who will find it helpful.

Measuring the Success of Your Content

I'm sure this one seems pretty obvious, but you need to track and measure the effectiveness of your content to truly understand what your audience is looking for.

Once you have a promotion plan for your content, measure its engagement in the form of impressions, conversions, video views, time on page, bounce rate, page views, engagement length, clicks, or any other metric that works for your type of content. These metrics should be able to paint a good picture of how valuable your audience finds your content and should also help you to identify the forms of content and length they prefer, as well as the medium they use to engage with the work.

Activity

Now that we've gone through the Helpful pillar, here are some initial steps you can take to create more impactful and helpful content for your audience:

1. Determine your target personas. If you have personas already, evaluate and expand them to incorporate as much detail as you can. The more detail you have, the better. Our goal should be to make our personas into people.

2. Do a content audit. If you have been in business more than a year, you likely have a lot of existing content you may have forgotten about or let fall through the cracks. In this audit, review the content for relevance, which

persona it is intended for, and which stage of the buyer's journey it correlates to. If a piece of content doesn't fit into a specific stage for a specific persona, either kill it or repurpose it.

3. Review your content to ensure that it's helpful and not overly salesy (when it's not called for). Each piece of content should have a logical next step for your audience and shouldn't immediately jump to a sales pitch, unless the next step is the decision stage.

4. Now that you have a clear idea of who your target personas are and what content already exists, determine holes in your content. What content is missing for which persona(s) in which stage(s)?

5. Create a full promotion plan for any new content aimed at your specific target personas.

6. Create a dashboard to measure the effectiveness of each piece of content. You should be able to identify which types of content, format, length, and medium each persona prefers to inform future content.

CHAPTER SEVEN

Community

The COVID-19 pandemic taught us many lessons, some that were entirely new and others that served more as reminders about what's important. And if isolation teaches you anything, it's that we crave community.

Even the most introverted person found themselves searching for others they could relate to during the depths of the pandemic — not to mention the desperate needs of going to the gym, getting a haircut, and just being out in public. Oh man…the hair, though.

Tapping into the power of community around your business, product, or service is equally important and allows customers to feel connected with your business and each other.

A great example of this is Peloton, the exercise and media company. When the COVID-19 pandemic closed gyms down, many people were forced to get their exercise at home and Peloton became hugely popular. You can see that in its Facebook group, which began in 2015 and grew to the point that the brand took over in 2017. When the pandemic hit in 2020, Peloton took advantage of the fact that their audience exponentially grew seemingly overnight. This significantly larger audience was starving for ways to keep up their fitness when nothing around them was open.[1]

As of this writing, the group sits at about 500,000 members and as Colin O'Riordan reported for HubSpot in 2020, "Peloton group members share personal biking stories, weight loss journeys, and offer each other advice. Engagement is so strong that any question posted is promptly answered by other members who act as advocates for the brand.

At the same time, Peloton diligently facilitates conversations and participates by asking members to share their progress in campaigns like their Fall Launch Challenge."[2]

As we can clearly see from Peloton, building a community around your brand, mission, vision, and audience is extremely valuable and lends itself to a more engaged, supported, and loyal audience. Let's examine a bit more.

The Power of Better Connectivity

Ever since social media became one of the (if not the) primary means of communication between people, scientists in a variety of fields have been examining the effects this has on a range of interpersonal relationships. And the results aren't good. Spending months and months isolated during a global pandemic certainly didn't help things.

Building a strong customer community requires active participation from your organization, so that's something you need to consider and plan for now and into the future.

While it may seem easy to just throw together a Facebook group and invite people in, you need to have a reason for your audience to join, a reason for them to stay, and most importantly — a reason for them to engage.

Your community, regardless of whether it lives on Facebook, LinkedIn, your website, or somewhere else, must be completely, 100% focused on your audience and supporting them. It should be an opportunity for your audience to engage with you and with others while getting their questions answered, finding inspiration and ideas, and forming bonds.

It's not going to happen quickly and it's not going to be successful if you just toss something out there without a plan. If you truly want to be successful in building a community, assign someone who thrives in social environments to lead this project and empower them to build the community from the ground up. Take the time, invest the resources, and keep it going. You're not going to see the return on investment immediately, but by building and nurturing this community, you'll reap those benefits for years to come.

When people feel like they are part of a community, they are more likely to engage with a business, product, or service on a much deeper level. That can lead to increased loyalty and advocacy for your business.

Get Customers Involved

Take a look at any number of the groups on Facebook centered around specific companies or products (or even the comments section on posts from brands) and you'll find people who are motivated to advocate for you to others, answer questions, and even provide product recommendations and troubleshooting. Word-of-mouth assistance and promotion is impactful and should be encouraged and fostered wherever and whenever possible.

Companies whose services or products are focused on specific hobbies or lifestyles can see real benefits from taking this kind of approach. It allows participants to do everything from arranging meetings or outings to troubleshooting and helping new members decide which products or services are best for them and why.

If you can find ways to involve your company — maybe through giveaways, contests, or recurring question and answer sessions — then you can provide members with the information and motivation they need to keep the community thriving.

Look at the work Nike did with its Run Club App, which has blossomed into an interactive space that encourages and accompanies runners out on the road. Along with more expected features like training and tracking, the app connects users to friends, family, and a larger community of fellow runners. It showcases just how vibrant a company-created community can be.[3]

Community as Business Resource

As I've covered at length in this book, customers connect with companies that are helpful. When trying to determine the information people come to you for, having a community that you can use as a resource will make your efforts much easier. It will also save you time and money on methods like surveys or digging through social media.

When customers feel like they're part of a community, they are more likely to share their thoughts and opinions openly because they feel as though what they think really matters, that they are supported, and that they're not the only one with their opinion. No one likes speaking up alone, so feeling like they have some back-up may make them more amenable to sharing their thoughts. It's scary to feel like you're alone or that you're the only one with a "dumb" question. By creating and nurturing a community, you can enable your audience to engage with others in similar situations with similar questions.

Demonstration of Commitment

It is easy to make claims, but showing actual follow through? That's how you win loyalty. If you're going to claim to be transparent and authentic, you need to show you mean it. As I've explained in the Transparency pillar, you need your customers to trust you. By building a community that fosters honest communication and sharing, you're demonstrating that your company means what it says. And in a crowded marketplace, where you need any advantage you can find, this might just be the crucial one.

All feedback isn't positive feedback and as much as we all want to hear about how great we and our company are and how people can't live without our products or services, there will be people that don't have those warm and fuzzy feelings. Be prepared for that. By creating a community, you're not only creating a forum for your advocates to talk about you, but you're also creating an opportunity for negative feedback. While I am not suggesting that you simply tolerate slander or someone trashing your company for the heck of it, you need to have a plan to engage with these people and respond.

Transparency means maintaining it through the good and the bad. No one is perfect and there are likely going to be complaints that arise (and they may not come up in the nicest or friendliest way).

Before you launch your community, have a plan and service level agreement in place for how quickly you will respond to comments or messages (both positive and negative), how you will handle the public communication of negative comments, and at what point your team will elevate issues to a supervisor or leader at your company.

One of the best ways to gain new customers is by handling negative feedback, reviews, or comments in a human, honest, and helpful way. Your audience understands that there are two sides to every story and that, well, there are plenty of jerks out there that are looking for any reason to publicly shame or bash a company.

By having a plan of how you will handle these comments and narratives, you will effectively manage a bad situation and you'll earn more trust and respect from your audience in the process.

Activity

Now that we've gone through the Community pillar, here are some impactful initial steps you can take to build a community around your brand:

1. Determine what platform (social media or otherwise) is most popular among your customers by sending out a survey that includes questions about which platforms they most use and why. Where do they interact with their friends and family? Where do they go to get information? Where do they get their shopping recommendations?

2. Work within your company to find someone who has experience with community management or look into hiring someone new.

3. Plan at least a month's worth of content for your pages, like giveaways, sponsored outings, questions, polls, and contests so you can build up consistency.

4. Create a group on the platform of choice and spread the word via your website, mail lists, and social media that there is a new group where people can join.

5. After a week of spreading the word about the community or after getting to a certain number of members, begin implementing your planned posts.

6. Create a service level agreement for how and
   when your team will manage and respond to
   new messages, comments, and threads.

   a. Be sure to include a well thought out
      plan for how to handle negative
      narratives and at what point will you get
      your leadership team involved.

[1] https://support.onepeloton.com/hc/en-us/articles/360039133051-Peloton-Challenges

[2] https://blog.hubspot.com/marketing/brands-growing-online-communities

[3] https://www.nike.com/nrc-app

CHAPTER EIGHT

The Solution

The ~~Sleazy~~ **New** Truth

We are past the time of the sleazy advertiser. This is the era of the helpful marketer who is focused on winning through education, being helpful, and connecting with their audience through building trust.

As we continue to empower the consumer, businesses must embrace the fact that they have the power and are doing their own research to find the companies, solutions, and tools they need to solve their problems and improve job performance.

The marketers who embrace this process are the marketers who are going to win and grow. The ones who rely on the old tactics of tricking and manipulating their audience to buy their product or service are going to be left in the dust.

As we move into the future, take the time to evaluate all your marketing campaigns and initiatives to determine if they are transparent, have personality, authenticity, consistency, are helpful, and encourage community.

It's important that we, as marketers, embrace the fact that we are not old-school advertisers and stop playing that role. We are not here to trick, manipulate, or persuade our audience to take action. We are here to help them make the right decision for their situation or business — and ideally that solution is to work with us. However, we also must embrace the fact that not every person or every business is the right fit for our offerings. We need to embrace and focus all of our efforts and energy on the right people — the people we help most. At the end of the day, the people we help and those we can make a true impact for are the people who will return, become advocates for us, and help us grow our businesses.

It's time we officially move out of that second stage of the spectrum of persuasion into rational and factual conversations that supports the needs of our

audience.

Table 1. *The spectrum of persuasion in advertising*

Coercition/Force	Manipulation	Rational persuasion	Factual information
Threat	Deceitful advertising	Logical arguments	Qualities
Physical violence	Fallacious arguments		Price
	Emotive persuasion		Display

Credit: Victor Danciu, Theoretical and Applied Economics 21.2 (2014): 591

~~More~~ **Better**, Always **Better**

The future of marketing and the future of our business

growth isn't in "more." It's in "better."

As we work to scale our organizations, the temptation

to solely focus on more — more leads, more dollars,

more website visits, more social followers, more

everything — is a danger to our success. Do we want

more dollars in our bank account? Absolutely. But by shifting our focus to better — better leads, better fit customers, better content, better user experience — we enable more money as a byproduct.

We are no longer marketers for SaaS companies, grocery stores, auto mechanics, insurance agencies, schools, programs, retailers, or any other industry.

No. We are educators. We are helpers. We are the reason our audiences make informed and accurate decisions. We are the reason our sales teams have great conversations with the right people when they're ready for those conversations.

Be an educator. Nothing is more important for a marketer.

~~Quantity-only~~ **Quality** Focus

A shift from the legacy quantity-only focus to a quality focus is not going to be an easy one. Leadership wants to see numbers. They want to see data. And they ALWAYS want to see that data trending in the right direction.

They want to see more leads coming in. They want to see growth in website traffic. They want to see more clicks and more social followers.

There will be a learning period within our organizations. We must reframe our roles and we must reframe our goals.

Instead of vanity metrics and quantity-only focused metrics (number of leads or website visits, etc.), we need to shift the focus to number of sales-qualified leads, number of meetings booked, deals created, impacted revenue, and repeat business. These metrics are focused on good quality, not just good volume.

The next time you set goals for your month, quarter, or year, take the time to assess whether those goals are quantity goals that could be reached by sleazy tactics or if they're quality-focused goals that will only be fulfilled by delivering the right information to the right people through the right methods at the right time.

We don't want more leads. We want more quality leads. We don't want more website traffic. We want more traffic from our ideal audiences.

Be picky. Be transparent about who your audience is. And center your entire strategy and content around these people. No more measuring your effectiveness as a marketer by the number of spam form fills that come in or the amount of irrelevant traffic you push to your website.

~~Lack of~~ **Regular** Educational Content

Content for the sake of content is a waste of time, but so is salesy content if you're putting it in front of your audience at the wrong time.

Like I said — we, as marketers, are educators. It's time we embrace that and lean into education.

To be effective educators, we must create content that meets our audience where they are in their buyer's journey, solves their problems, answers their questions, and gives them a next step in the process.

Build a content calendar and stick to it. We should be looking to create more than 50 new pieces of helpful content in all three stages of the buyer's journey (awareness, consideration, and decision) on a monthly basis between blog posts, website copy, emails, social media posts, flyers, downloadable content, and any other form of content you can share with your audience.

Remember — this is all in addition to your sales content. That lives in a separate bucket and should be reserved for the audience that is ready for it. We shouldn't be hitting our awareness or consideration stage contacts with any sales messaging.

~~Overly~~ **Strategically** Gated Content

Let's be clear, I am not against gating content. I think it is a valuable and effective way to create leads that can be nurtured to become sales-qualified leads.

However, I have some very big "buts..." that accompany that statement.

Gating should be reserved for only the largest, most important, and impactful content. If you have more than a dozen pieces of gated content, you're probably going too far. Examples of appropriate gated materials include: heavy research pieces, templates, tools, and impactful items your audience should be able to immediately extract value from or put into practice.

Gating anything other than these items should be immediately reconsidered.

For example, HIVE has a client we worked with on the rebuild and relaunch of their website. They have a great business that focuses on eliminating car emissions and reducing the amount of fuel burned. This does a lot of good for their customers' bottom line, as well as the environment.

On their website they have a savings calculator that helps their audience understand the impact using their services can have on their clients' fleets. It's a great tool that provides a lot of insight, but it was gated. Who is willing to give up their information for a tool that tells you what *could* happen?

The calculator is an innovative tool and can leave an impression, especially in the decision stage of their audience's buyer's journey, but the benefit is truly for the business. It's an opportunity to show their audience how great the solution is. It's not helpful in their audience's research of how to reduce CO_2 emissions.

Now that we've relaunched their website, it's ungated and has turned from a sales tool to an educational marketing tool.

The form used to gate your content should also be proportional to the value your audience receives but should also never exceed five to seven fields. For example, if you have a useful eBook that helps your audience in the awareness stage to understand their problems, you should only be asking for an email (and maybe one or two other pieces of non-sensitive information). If something is super valuable to your audience, like a full-blown research paper or proprietary tool, asking for a few more pieces of information is acceptable.

Far too often, we see organizations ask for the world in exchange for basic content that isn't all that helpful.

Cut your forms back. Only ask for information that is necessary to continue to be helpful for your audience. The less you require, the more conversions you'll get and the more likely you'll be to start a relationship with the right audience.

"Bad" Targeted Leads

I am very excited to put "bad" leads to rest. Instead, we are focused on providing more targeted, higher quality leads to our sales teams.

This starts with the fact that not every lead that comes through should be immediately pushed to sales. In fact, very few of the overall leads that come into your pipeline should reach sales (at least right away).

It's time to do more work on the front end and focus on nurturing the leads that come in, engage with them, follow and help them, and when they have signaled that they're ready for that sales conversation, then pass them to your sales team.

We do a lot of HubSpot onboardings and implementations and many of them come with a needed integration to Salesforce because their sales team uses Salesforce and will continue to do so. One of the biggest requests we get is to push all contacts that come in over to Salesforce so the sales team can reach out.

Let me get this straight — you're telling me the person who subscribed to your blog is ready for a salesperson to reach out to them? Or the person who filled out a form to get your awareness or consideration stage content is expecting to hear from your salesperson? They're not. This is why we all have such anxiety about filling out any forms on any website.

Be better.

Be better about providing the experience your audience is expecting.

Be better about nurturing your leads and helping them move throughout their buyer's journey.

Be better about identifying and qualifying leads long before they get to a salesperson.

The Future of Marketing

Now, after reading this book, you may be wondering, "Dustin, what about the future of marketing? What about artificial intelligence?"

I'm glad you asked. In fact, this exact conversation came up amongst my leadership team as I was finishing this book.

I brought up ChatGPT to my leadership team and mentioned that we as an agency need to be investing in AI to be more efficient in our processes and eliminate unnecessary time in creating content.

Mallory, my Director of Marketing Operations, stopped in her tracks and said, "Wait — you're writing a book called *Market Like A Human* and now you're telling us that we should be using artificial intelligence?"

It was a great question. I fully believe AI is going to have a massive impact on most industries, including marketing. But I also think the concept of AI taking over has been blown way out of proportion. It is becoming a solution to streamlining processes, building a foundation, and starting a project. It is becoming a viable and useful tool for content and sales teams to speed up and increase their output. Not a solution to eliminate the need to create. Not a solution to eliminate the need for a marketer. And not a replacement to connect with our audience.

In a conversation I had with Paul Roetzer, Founder and CEO of the Marketing Artificial Intelligence Institute, he shared his company's belief and tag line, "More Intelligent. More Human.™" Roetzer sees artificial intelligence as a way to, "Free us up from the repetitive tasks humans don't enjoy so we can work on the things we're passionate about."

Roetzer went on to share an example of how he is using AI in his business (which is obviously centered around AI). They run an "Intro to AI for Marketers" live class[1] regularly, with hundreds of marketers in attendance. Through that event, the company collects a lot of leads they then reach out to manually on LinkedIn — yes, manually. By a human.

He explained, "Someone on my team reaches out to every person who registers for the events personally on LinkedIn to thank them for attending and to offer support and answer questions. We do it all manually with no AI involved. We are able to do that because we use artificial intelligence to take other tasks off of our plates to free up time to have that very human interaction."

See, the concept of *Market Like A Human* is not about who is creating the content, who had the idea, or who is doing what part of the process. It's about how we can create a better experience for the humans we market to. We're never going to be marketing to AI. We are *always* going to be marketing to human beings. It doesn't matter where the content comes from or if you decide to use AI. It matters how we use them to be better marketers for our audience. If that means taking basic tasks off our plates to free up time, great. If that means the AI is going to help us in topic creation, image generation, outlines, drafts, summarization, transcription, video creation, or any of the thousands of potential use cases, also great.

AI is a new(er) and more advanced tool to help get the job done. It's a new way to help us connect.

Roetzer also added a word of warning around the ways in which AI should be used: "The biggest challenge right now is most executives don't understand AI, but they're starting to make decisions based on misconceptions about what they think AI is."

He went on to give an example of one of the many scenarios that could play out.

"A Chief Marketing Officer may start playing around with ChatGPT and think they can replace their writers with this tool when in reality, they're meant to work together. Instead, that CMO should think about utilizing AI and keep the same staff to increase output. There is a lot of pressure to learn AI and implement it quickly right now, but it needs to be done in an ethical way."

The Marketing AI Institute's manifesto[2] for businesses is to be more transparent (hey, another *Market Like A Human* pillar) with their audience about their use of AI in their business and campaigns.

I encourage everyone to explore how AI can impact their workflow, eliminate writer's block, speed up processes, and create more impactful content. But remember, AI shouldn't be viewed as a replacement for human marketers. The Marketing AI Institute's manifesto states, "AI technologies should be assistive, not autonomous." Use them together, humans and AI. Empower your marketing team to use every tool at their disposal (including artificial intelligence) to better connect with your audience and always continue to better *Market Like A Human*.

Activities

Thank you for taking this journey with me and for your efforts in creating a more human marketing industry. As we have now gone through all the pillars of *Market Like A Human*, here are the activities associated with each you can use to start taking meaningful steps towards being a more human-centric marketer and engage with your audience on a deeper, more trust-filled level.

The Problem

1. Pull together a list of your goals for this month, quarter, and/or year and think about how you can improve them so they're more heavily focused on quality than quantity.

    a. If you're part of a larger team, discuss with the entire group what a transition to a quality-focus looks like and how you can incorporate that into your marketing and sales expectations moving forward.

2. Run a content audit to determine how much of your content is sales-focused versus helpful.

    a. Additionally, ascertain how much of your content is gated and how much you're asking for from your users. Think about what could be ungated, what could be repurposed, and which forms you may be able to reduce to lower the barrier to entry.

3. Review your form process to determine how and when a lead is being sent to a salesperson and determine whether that lead would be expecting, or even ready for, a sales conversation, or if they were just looking for helpful resources.

4. Talk with your sales team to determine why the leads they're being delivered are "bad" and how you can improve the quality of those leads.

5. Review some impactful marketing campaigns that you've seen recently, whether in your industry or that you've seen as a consumer, and determine what you liked and didn't like about the campaigns and content.

    a. Once you've reviewed these campaigns as a team, brainstorm how you could implement something similar for your organization's campaigns and how it can impact and resonate with the humans that you're marketing to.

Transparency

1. Make a list of questions your sales team gets in the sales process and create content to answer those (even the difficult or uncomfortable ones).
2. Add pricing information to your website and make it easy to find.
       a. This can be in the form of straight-forward pricing details, a pricing

calculator, table, or even just a range of costs.

    i. If you are using a range, be sure to include information about what impacts overall costs.

3. Run a search through Answer the Public (answerthepublic.com) to find questions your audience is asking and create content around those questions. This can be in the form of blog posts, videos, social media posts, website pages, email, and more.

Personality

1. Talk to your team (including everyone from executives to interns) to better understand their personalities. Incorporating your team's

personality into your campaigns will make the
content feel more authentic and impactful.

2. Take stock of the content you have produced
    in the past and review for personality. What is
    the tone and theme of this content? Did it
    resonate with your target audience? Could you
    incorporate more personality into a revision of
    this content?

3. Review your competitors' personalities. How
    can you stand out in comparison by
    incorporating more (or a different) personality?

Authenticity

1. Review your content for any explicit or implicit
    promises and ensure you have a plan to follow
    through on those promises. It's always better

to under promise and over deliver than the other way around.

2. Eliminate any barriers or constraints you have around your industry or your business. You don't have to fit a mold. Determine who you are and who you want to be as a company and own it.

3. Share the causes you believe in, as well as how you are supporting them and how others can get involved. Even if your causes aren't directly related to your organization, share them with your audience. It will make your organization feel more human and will build an immense amount of trust.

   a. If there aren't any social causes that you currently support, do some

research and see how your
organization can get involved in your
community. It doesn't need to be
monetary involvement. Encourage your
team to volunteer, spread the word, or
even do some pro bono work. There
are many ways to get involved in your
community.

4. If you have someone at your organization who
    is comfortable on camera, make a plan to go
    live at least once per month on the social
    networks that make sense for your target
    audience. Most social media platforms today
    offer some version of live streaming for users
    and businesses.

5. Share real customer stories in your marketing campaigns. No one likes to be first when it comes to working with an organization. Prospects want to know that others have done it and succeeded. Share social proof and case studies to help your campaigns and company to feel more genuine and relatable.

6. Review all your content for language and voice. If your messaging is overly salesy, rewrite it to be more helpful and authentic. Use your own voice and language to better connect with your audience.

7. Your mission and vision should be at the heart of all your decisions. Straying away from these core values can make your company feel inauthentic and disingenuous. Review every

decision, campaign, and piece of content through the lens of your organization's mission and vision statements.

Consistency

1. Create a brand guide and stick to it. Your brand is everything and needs to be protected. You can start a brand guide by using tools like Brand Folder (brandfolder.com), Brandtools (brand.tools), and even Canva (canva.com), among many others. It's important to have a documented brand guide that is shared throughout your organization so that everyone is using your brand in an appropriate way.

2. Use real photos and videos wherever possible. Using real photos and videos in your

campaigns, rather than stock images or staged footage makes your campaigns feel more authentic, genuine, and consistent.

3. Create a content calendar and stick to it. As you create your calendar, think about what stage of the buyer's journey your audience is in, which of your target personas care most about each piece of content, your audience's preferred medium for receiving and engaging with your work, and what the next step in their journey will be.

4. Recruit help. Many organizations lack the necessary resources to get content created and published and often it falls on one person, which is just a recipe for disaster. Recruit help from within your organization or tap into

outside resources to ensure you stick to your content plan and deliver the consistent content search engines and audiences crave.

Helpful

1. Determine your target personas. If you have personas already, evaluate and expand them to incorporate as much detail as you can. The more detail you have, the better. Our goal should be to make our personas into people.

2. Do a content audit. If you have been in business more than a year, you likely have a lot of existing content you may have forgotten about or let fall through the cracks. In this audit, review the content for relevance, which persona it is intended for, and which stage of

the buyer's journey it correlates to. If a piece of content doesn't fit into a specific stage for a specific persona, either kill it or repurpose it.

3. Review your content to ensure that it's helpful and not overly salesy (when it's not called for). Each piece of content should have a logical next step for your audience and shouldn't immediately jump to a sales pitch, unless that is the next step in the decision stage.

4. Now that you have a clear idea of who your target personas are and what content already exists, determine holes in your content. What content is missing for which persona(s) in which stage(s)?

5. Create a full promotion plan for any new content aimed at your specific target personas.

6. Create a dashboard to measure the effectiveness of each piece of content. You should be able to identify which types of content, format, length, and medium each persona prefers to inform future content.

Community

1. Determine what platform (social media or otherwise) is most popular among your customers by sending out a survey that includes questions about which platforms they most use and why: Where do they interact with their friends and family? Where do they go to get information? Where do they get their shopping recommendations?

2. Work within your company to find someone who has experience with community management or look into hiring someone new.

3. Plan at least a month's worth of content for your pages, like giveaways, sponsored outings, questions, polls, and contests so you can build up consistency.

4. Create a group on the platform of choice and spread the word via your website, mail lists, and social media that there is a new group where people can join.

5. After a week of spreading the word about the community or after getting to a certain number of members, begin implementing your planned posts.

6. Create a service level agreement for how and when your team will manage and respond to new messages, comments, and threads.

   a. Be sure to include a well thought out plan for how to handle negative narratives and at what point will you get your leadership team involved.

[1] https://www.marketingaiinstitute.com/intro-to-ai-for-marketers

[2] https://www.marketingaiinstitute.com/blog/the-responsible-ai-manifesto-for-marketing-and-business

Acknowledgements

I am a firm believer that nothing worth doing ever gets done alone. We all have amazing support systems made up of advocates, colleagues, family, friends, and acquaintances that make our success possible. This book and its completion are no different.

The idea of *Market Like A Human* came to me through interactions with clients and competitive research for them. I noticed there was a lack of humanity in marketing and if we and our clients wanted to grow, we had to take a new approach. We had to make a shift from a quantity focus to a quality focus. We realized we needed to act to become more human.

What a concept. Through all that work, this book was born.

Over the course of many hours researching, writing, and editing — plus my team at HIVE Strategy having to hear me say *Market Like A Human* on repeat for a year — we came up with a book that I am so proud to share with the world. I would like to acknowledge some of the many people that made this all possible.

Clarke Reader, you, sir, are an absolute wordsmith and I am so grateful that you were by my side throughout this project. Your contributions were so very valuable. We would never have published without you. Thank you so much. I can't wait to work with you on future iterations and books.

To the team at HIVE Strategy — specifically Yvonne Hall, Mallory Fetchu, Michael Thebeau, Jill Schneider, Amber Bolusan, Chris Queen, Mason Yarber, Evan Burns, Matt Louden, Alejandro Rodriguez, Tymire Garner, Melissa Samaroo, Desiree Landa, and Hilary Sperley — thank you so much for supporting me on this journey and helping to push it forward. You all are the best team I could ever ask for and I value and appreciate each of you more than you know.

To Chris Savage of Wistia, Paul Roetzer of Marketing AI Institute, and William Todd, author of *The Mentor In Me*, I appreciate you taking time out of your busy schedules to share your insights, knowledge, and wisdom with me. Thank you for your contributions and for guiding the *Market Like A Human* mission forward through your own processes, ideas, and beliefs. Keep doing amazing things, the world needs you.

And finally, to my amazing personal support system — Laura Brackett, Bailey Brackett, Kathy Brackett, Deborah Platt, David Platt, Andrea Carlton, Jessica Carlton, Kristen Carlton, Dawn Basko, Marie Zimmerman, Amber Klein, Adam Scott, Omar Ortiz, Amber Page-Ortiz, Hank Glackin, and Kelley Glackin — thank you for always supporting my crazy ideas, pushing me to be my best self, and believing in me, even when I don't. I couldn't have done any of this without such an amazing support system. Thank you all from the bottom of my heart.

About the Author

Dustin Brackett

———————————

In a world full of noise, empty promises, and sleazy marketing tactics, Dustin is on a mission to change the industry perception and to help organizations reach their audience and consumers on a more human level. Through the tactics and methodologies in *Market Like A Human*, Dustin believes we can all be better, more engaging marketers who do good for the world.

Dustin is an entrepreneur and a 15-year marketing industry veteran and founded his first agency in 2014, called Bee Social, which eventually grew into HIVE Strategy, an inbound marketing agency and current Diamond HubSpot Solutions Partner. Through his time as an entrepreneur and marketing executive, he has run the gamut of testing, trials, successes, and failures to help to establish his *Market Like A Human* philosophy and methodology for his agency and clients.

HIVE Strategy works with medium to enterprise business-to-business brands whose goal is educating and connecting with their audiences through trust building and relationships. Most HIVE clients are in the technology, education, consulting, finance, and health and wellness spaces, and are HubSpot users. If you're interested in a consultation or learning more about how HIVE Strategy can support your organization's growth goals, visit www.hivestrategy.com.

But HIVE was not the perfect fit for everyone that needed help, so Dustin launched HIVE Hub, a fractional HubSpot admin and HubSpot task management service that works with HubSpot users and agencies to execute and deliver on HubSpot tasks. If you're in need of HubSpot support, please visit www.gohivehub.com.

Dustin resides in Denver, Colorado, with his beautiful wife, Laura, their daughter, Bailey, and their dogs, Arrow and Kobe.

Thank you for taking the time to read my book. I hope that you found it insightful and that you're leaving with at least a few ideas to make your organization more human-centric in your marketing initiatives. Please connect with me and keep the conversation going. I'd love to hear from you and see how you are employing the *Market Like A Human* philosophy to your own marketing.

Contact Information

Email: dustin@marketlikeahuman.com

LinkedIn: linkedin.com/in/dbrackett

Twitter: @dbrackett88

Web: www.hivestrategy.com

www.gohivehub.com

www.marketlikeahuman.com